INDONESIA IS A HAPPENING

INDONESIA

IS A HAPPENING

by

Christopher Lucas

with photographs by Victor Englebert

A WEATHERHILL BOOK

WALKER / WEATHERHILL : *New York & Tokyo*

Excerpts from this book originally appeared in *Venture*.
The author gratefully acknowledges the magazine's
kind permission for the present use of the material.

First edition, 1970

Published by JOHN WEATHERHILL, INC., *of New York and Tokyo, with
editorial offices at 7-6-13 Roppongi, Minato-ku, Tokyo 106. Distributed
in the United States by* WALKER AND COMPANY, *720 Fifth Avenue, New
York City 10019. Copyright © 1970 by Christopher Lucas; all rights re-
served. Printed in Japan.*

LCC Card No. 77-121067   *IS BN 0-8027-2441-8*

FOR GIOVANNA

CONTENTS

PHOTOGRAPHS

INDONESIA IS A HAPPENING

"You'd say I'm putting you on. But it's no joke."
—THE BEATLES

. . . as I was saying, I went to Indonesia by mistake. Like I got trapped. It was the hour before dawn in Tokyo, then the phone jangled, and it's New York calling, sir, and there's a honey-hard woman's voice asking don't I really want to go to Indonesia. So I hang up and climb back into bed. Three months later the honey-hard voice is back, and this time she's in Tokyo and no messing around. The lady's in public relations and she's got a product. Indonesia. All 735,865 square miles. She's also got a suite in Wright's old Imperial Hotel, where she clobbers me with pamphlets and brochures and promises of sybaritic living. I'll be a guest of the Generals, she keeps suggesting, pampered like royalty, blandished with cars, courtesans, and other exotic goodies. And anyway, General Suharto is such a lovely man, isn't he? The executive lady wears plunging necklines like Joan Crawford used to. She's also insistent as hell. She calls me five times a day, flatters, cajoles, finally perjures me into saying I'll maybe go. She's got me squirming, beaten, out of excuses. I want to go to Angkor, Manáos, Burundi, even Katmandu. But Djakarta, never. Next morning there's an air ticket in the mailbox. TYO-DJA-TYO. So what do you do? . . .

THE SCENE

1 Balok the Hunter is snoring. He killed a black leopard today and the raw hide is pinned to our bedroom wall. It smells dreadful. Balok skewered the brute with his rusty old spear, then cut its throat. Huddled in a batik cloth, the hunter now tosses and twitches on the hard ground, and sometimes smiles in his sleep. Maybe he's dreaming how he gouged the leopard's eyes, then threw them to his half-starved mongrels. Anyway, he looks happy. And as he slumbers, Balok gingerly cradles a Soviet machine-pistol. A 75-round Stechkin. He is my bodyguard, after all.

We're sitting on a hot volcano, tippling pink soda pop, and catching the late-late show, a *wayang kulit*. But Balok is too tired to care, and so am I. It's 4 A.M.

The oil lamps gutter and spit. Under the tangled reaches of a gigantic banyan, the villagers perch cross-legged, mesmerized by Amir the Storyteller. His ritual chants drone eerily across the jungle slope, and high above the palms, wrapped in a swirl of sulphurous vapors, the volcanic cone glows amber. My god! It's all so beautiful, and so damn weird. I feel edgy, shiftless, out of it. Time has stopped.

The shadow play began eight long hours ago, just after nightfall, and will end two hours after dawn. Or will it? So I splice my soda pop from the hip flask, and impatiently kick Amir's pet pythons. Coiled in oozing, scaly heaps, these two bloated, obscene monsters stir in their bamboo cage, then slither and unwind, like living hawsers. They're not my favorite companions, but I'm a guest.

Rather improbably, we're celebrating the fifteenth anniversary of Indonesia's marine corps, but General Suharto's fine words got lost in the mail. So did his color portrait and the crisp, new red-and-white flag. Our host is also missing, but the stoic tribesmen don't give a damn. They're much too busy smoking pot, frying bean curd, minding babies, and savoring Amir's hypnotic spell.

For the storyteller draws them far from the painful present. In his ten-hour tour de force, the *dalang* masterfully embroiders the ancient legends of the *Ramayana*. He keeps six cutout puppets moving and talking at the same time, and as their shadows flicker across a grimy linen screen, the village's own gamelan punctuates the courtly battles and romances. Squatting in a circle, the turbaned musicians haphazardly strike their clutter of gongs and bamboo xylophones, then roll another joint.

Balok wakes brusquely and sits up. His eyes flit suspiciously.

"Many spirits about tonight," he says darkly. "Yes, the puppets are possessed. Amir makes strong magic."

I half smile.

"Don't laugh," says Balok. "Spirits very dangerous."

Balok, who catches pythons with his hands, looks up warily into the banyan's rustling branches.

"This tree holds most terrible *demit*," he whispers. "One night he put broken glass my wife's belly. Wife now very dead!"

Balok quaffs a comforting jigger of Scotch, thanks me, then moodily wipes his Stechkin. The musicians pause. In the distance, there's the chatter of monkeys, and fireflies hover. It's very still.

Suddenly a bloodcurdling howl splits the night. Balok jerks around, finger on trigger. Then we laugh. It is no demon after all. It's our host Alidin, a bouncy, crew-cut marine ensign. He's been off whoring, and although it's the first day of Ramadan, the Muslims' month of abstinence, he's unspeakably, rip-roaring drunk. He's also nine hours late.

Weaving between the villagers, Alidin clutches five huge

coconuts, pitches and rolls like a storm-tossed cockleshell; and
after an off-key chorus of *Indonesia Raya,* the national anthem,
he flops into the chair next to mine. He rips off his camouflage
jacket, tosses away his pistol holster, and draws a mean-looking
machete. He splits a coconut and, with mock ceremony, hands
me the milk-filled husk.

"We are the New Forces!" he roars. "Everybody welcome
in Indonesia. Even bloody Dutchmen!"

And he collapses in helpless laughter.

Balok smiles sheepishly, and a wrinkled old lady tactfully removes the baby she'd placed on my lap hours before. But Amir
the Storyteller keeps talking. The drummer raps his tom-tom
with a clenched fist, and the show goes on. After all, the Baluran
Game Reserve is hardly the place for political debate.

Stranded on the east tip of Java, I've inexplicably mislaid my
jeep, my suitcase, and maybe my sanity. We are 53 miles from
Panarokan, which is 110 miles from Surabaya, which is 600 miles
from Djakarta, which is 10,000 light-years from New York. For
the innocent-at-large, it's the end of the road; but it takes more
than an inebriated marine to disturb the aplomb of centuries.

Ignored by the tribesmen, Alidin empties my hip flask into
his coconut, slurps it down in one gulp. He rolls his eyes, belches
loudly, then throws a flaccid arm around me.

"You my friend, *tuan,*" he mumbles mawkishly. "Why you
not go see my girl? She give you good time. Only twenty-five
cents."

I tell Alidin it's 5:15 A.M., but thank him all the same. My
host shakes his head ruefully, lurches to his feet, props himself
against the magic banyan, and urinates. Allah be praised.

Across the way, a wild boar abruptly flushes three squawking
peacocks from the jungle. Poised on the clearing's edge, tusks
dipped like lances, the bristling killer stands snorting and confused. Yet the villagers keep their torpid cool. It's bad manners
to show panic. Balok rolls over on one elbow, squeezes off a
dozen rounds of tracer, and the wild boar turns tail.

"Dirty pig!" says Balok.

The shadowy puppets keep dancing, the gamelan strikes up
a vague, languorous dirge, and I flick another black leech off my

ankle. Alidin slumps limply into his canvas chair. With one hand, he fumbles in his khaki pouch, then pulls out his proudest possession. A pocket tape recorder. Grinning foolishly, Alidin hangs it around his neck, inserts a cassette, and drowns our tranquil slope with alien, fiendish sound. The Rolling Stones, no less.

The tribesmen huddle indifferently, and as Alidin drifts into deepest, drunken sleep, the sudden dawn of the tropics breaks once again, flushing purple, mauve, then coral pink.

I have not slept for three days. I haven't had a square meal in two weeks. And I begin to wonder. What the hell am I doing here anyway?

■ **2** ■ Indonesia isn't a country, it's a happening. If the hippies only knew, it's the ultimate total experience, as unpredictable as a fistful of mercury. It's a script written by Conrad, Kafka, and Edgar Allan Poe, with a helping hand from Marx—Groucho, that is. It's a scene with more hangups than reason will buy or logic condone. Maybe it's just a put-on, after all. But Indonesia isn't saying.

It's a land where the *komodo* lizard grows ten feet long, where offices close at 2 P.M. and never reopen, where oranges swell like footballs, where people say "yes" when they mean "maybe." It's a land where Christians worship rocks; where inflation can hit 650 percent a year; where worms are a delicacy; where generals earn $100 a month, then splurge $60,000 on a daughter's wedding. It's a land where a nice family means fifteen children; where trains stop for evening prayers; where the right persons turn up at the wrong place at the right time and vice versa. It's a land where 300,000 get massacred, and the people shrug. "We live in the fifth dimension," says a Swiss resident, slightly perplexed. "This is strictly *Through the Looking Glass* country."

Indonesia can frustrate, irritate, and infuriate, yet eventually she seduces even the most jaundiced, as she has done since time began. The Chinese, the Indians, the Arabs, the phlegmatic Dutch—they've all succumbed. There's a quicksand quality to Indonesia. Like a beautiful woman, she can act spoiled, elusive, and foully arrogant; yet when she does finally give herself, she makes the waiting worthwhile. Or so I'm told. Above all, she is beautiful—outrageously so. She has temperament, mystery, and devastating charm. She's also a complex bitch.

Both violent and docile, exuberant and apathetic, Indonesia can be exciting and tedious, passionate and puritan, practical yet superstitious, incomparably stable yet incurably volatile. In short, she's the homeland of paradox.

By any yardstick, the Republic of Indonesia, which inherited the world's fifth-biggest population, is a unique proposition. Scattered across the equator, the archipelago's 13,667 islands stretch almost 3,500 miles, the distance between New York and London, and are inhabited by 117 million people, who represent forty-three different racial types, speak two hundred different languages, and practice seven different religions. It's no coincidence that the national motto should be a cliff-hanging "Unity in Diversity."

In this mind-blowing tumult, the anthropologist can juggle time itself, identify *genus biped* at every stage of civilization, and stop off anywhere between the Stone Age and the Space Age.

In the remote highlands of West Irian, the dour, negroid tribes wear bones through their noses, use cowrie shells for money, carve stone tips for their arrows. In Borneo's rain forests, the notorious Dayak still hunt a head or two; and in Sumatra's outback, a wife can be bought for thirty pigs, or less.

In the villages of Bali, the honey-skinned peasants till their rice paddies with wooden plows, barter pigs for cloth, placate cruel Shiva with medieval apprehension. And from the distant Celebes, intrepid Lascar seamen thrust their crescent-sailed *prahu* across the empty oceans like their pirate fathers.

In the surging townships of Java, adipose Chinese merchants now sprawl across the counters of the squat, eighteenth-century godowns built by the Dutch colonials, while in the capital of Djakarta the young executive roars off on a motor scooter. His briefcase holds a Gideon Bible and a diploma from M.I.T.

There's no happy catch phrase for Indonesia. Ten plus one still equals nine.

JAVA

1 I've been chewing my nails for six days in Djakarta, waiting for a general who promised a car. Within hours, they keep saying, I'll be sweeping through the scenic wonders of Java, en route for Bali. But my general has flitted to San Francisco, his aides have vaporized, and every other general has either gone to Buenos Aires, Milan, Tokyo, or simply isn't there. I spend my mornings drifting through bleak offices where the clerks smile sadly. In present-day Indonesia, it's worth knowing, Generals are the only people who get things done, and motor cars are scarcer than hens' teeth. "So why not play golf?" they keep asking.

It's hot, humid, and my shirt is soaked. I've got stomach cramps, insomnia, and I'm getting nowhere. I'm bogged in promises, up to my eyeballs. And I wish I'd never come.

Regrettably, Djakarta is the unavoidable port of entry into Indonesia. As Paris isn't France, however, Djakarta isn't Indonesia, which is fortunate. For the capital is a fiasco. Its steaming, scruffy Kemajoran Airport is probably the most depressing on earth. There's nowhere to sit, the walls perspire, confusion is total, and the more timorous visitors get urges to board the next outgoing flight. And the city itself, at first glance, seems to offer all the more dubious exotica of Calcutta or Mao's Canton.

Besides malodorous canals where naked boys paddle, besides corrugated boulevards, dust-caked palms, and the stifling heat, Djakarta also has an exploding population, murky slums, and the other sores of poverty. From horizon to horizon, nestling between clumps of bamboo and blazing flamboyants, the flaking shacks and houses, still implausibly roofed with ruddy Dutch tiles, stretch to eternity. "It's a village which has split at the seams," says a Dutch old-timer. "Four million people in search of a city planner."

After a few days' exploration, however, Djakarta does hold a certain perverse fascination. Once known as Batavia, it was the proud capital of the Netherlands East Indies until 1949. Then independence struck and the rot began. These days, the thriving Dutch capital has lapsed into faded, bankrupt splendor; so has the vainglorious Djakarta of Sukarno.

It's a disquieting sensation. My first morning, I wasn't sure whether the city had been hit by a hydrogen bomb or a building boom. Actually, it was neither. Across Djakarta, towering steel skeletons, their girders rusting, prod the sky; whole acres of cement and empty scaffolding stand ready for hotels and office blocks; the extravagant framework of a vast mosque looks particularly forlorn. These are the half-completed follies of Sukarno, the fallen demagogue, whose more practical heirs have blocked all his swollen-headed schemes and prefer to spend what's left on filling potholes and balancing the nightmare budget.

After two decades' neglect by President Sukarno, who squandered billions on colossal stadiums, conference halls, and Soviet-styled statuary, the once-trim squares carved out by the Dutch are rank with weeds, scrawny goats and heifers graze between the neglected flower beds, and barefoot peddlers trundle their handcarts down crumbling, midtown sidewalks. At strategic corners, Sukarno's monumental eyesores—the workers rending their chains, freedom fighters locked in everlasting battle—still flaunt their Marxist, and distinctly obsolete, iconography. Big-

Indonesia's beauty can be breathtakingly melodramatic. In remote East Java, a clutch of mysterious, smoking volcanoes looms above the clouds. On the horizon, the brooding hulk of Mount Bromo. Tribesmen propitiate the demons within by tossing live bulls into the crater. There are more than four hundred volcanoes in Indonesia, and many still rumble ominously. Remember Krakatoa? It made the biggest bang since Pompeii, and killed 35,000. Its explosion was heard 2,500 miles away. ▶

gest of all, the National Monument is a gold-tipped obelisk which rises 330 feet from an apparent soup bowl and is irreverently known as "Sukarno's last erection."

"Three years ago Djakarta was a dead city," I was told repeatedly. "Now at least it wants to live again." Maybe. Djakarta today proudly boasts its first department store, the fourteen-story Sarinah, complete with an improbable roof-top casino. Thamrin Avenue, the capital's Main Street, is finally being repaved, and even the British, whose embassy was fired and ransacked by Sukarno's hoodlums, have seen fit to finance a handsome replacement. I'd hardly call the mood optimistic, but the ghosts have been exorcised, and the house cleaning has begun.

There's an impressive new motorway which goes nowhere in particular, half a dozen new office complexes for government penpushers, and a mushrooming slice of suburbia known as Kebajoran Baru, where the bungalows are spruce and the lawns get sprinkled. Even the venerable Djakarta Museum, which owns a musty but priceless collection of Chinese ceramics, has been given a dust-up. Which didn't inhibit the watchman from telling me, one hour before closing, that I'd, please, better go. "The museum isn't full enough," he said.

After the xenophobic years of abandon, Djakarta has also won back the confidence to recognize and restore the heirlooms of Holland. President Suharto and his generals suffer no complexes about the past. Once the Dutch governor-general's residence, the gracious Merdeka Palace, with its fluted columns, colonial facade, and chandeliers on the portico, has had a fresh coat of paint, as have the stolid, Dutch-built ministries (run by Gener-

◄ *Whatever the Generals say, art and religion are still the bloodstream of Indonesia. They help make chaos coherent.* ABOVE: *Framed by huge, bell-shaped stupas, a meditating, unusually youthful Buddha stares cooly from the summit of Borobudur, the country's greatest Buddhist monument. The girl in slacks is also having a quiet think.* BELOW: *The gaudy panache of wayang wong, Java's most popular theater form. The Hindu god Shiva, played by a woman, retains her ritual cool while being taunted by bearded devils and other underworld creatures. As usual, the story is drawn from the Hindu classic the* Mahabharata. *And Shiva triumphs.*

als), the Dutch-built banks (run by Generals), and the better Dutch-built homes (run by Generals' wives).

■ **2** ■ All in all, there's a prevalence of Generals, and it's a fact of life that they run the country. President Suharto, who dumped Sukarno into political limbo, is after all a military man. He trusts the tools of his trade, and in a country where corruption is endemic, he also trusts his own men above others. Whether his confidence is reciprocated—well, that's none of my business. Unlike his predecessor, Suharto does, however, like law and order, and he makes his intentions both clear and visible. He has 360,000 troops fully mobilized, keeps armored cars and 50-mm cannon parked at every university campus, and when the fancy strikes him, rumbles a squadron of Soviet-made heavy tanks through town. As a reminder.

By my tastes, there are rather too many troops around for comfort. Yet the military presence isn't suffocating, just ubiquitous, and most Djakarta citizens, who remember the grisly bloodletting of 1965, accept it all with engaging fatalism. Like my friend Karim. "Suharto? Sukarno? What's the damn difference?" he asks. "The average Indonesian still earns less than thirty-four dollars a year and dies before he's thirty-two." And as our springless old Hillman shudders into gear, the laconic Karim, a university lecturer with damp sideburns and a Zapata mustache, throws us into frontal conflict with Djakarta's traffic.

Chewing an unlit cheroot, Karim plunges straight into a swarm of *betjak*, the gaudy, painted tricycles that serve as taxis. The *betjak* scatter. We miss an oncoming buffalo cart by inches, swerve around a stalled bus, graze a cyclist who's balancing six terra-cotta pots on his head, jump an open sewer, and finally grind to a halt on the sidewalk. Karim barely has time to point out a grim, gray-washed fortress. Its high walls fairly bristle with broken glass. "That's the jail," he gasps. "It's packed with Communists. Three years ago, it was packed with anti-Communists." And we're off again.

With reckless bravado, Karim dodges through an impossible maze of narrow streets. The pavements are crammed with stalls,

and in the swirl of dust and exhaust fumes, the owners nonchalantly build their pyramids of mangoes, wrap a stick of root
ginger or cinnamon bark, pour a jigger of rice wine. A para-
trooper dozes against a tree, his pink beret drawn over his eyes,
Impervious to the prowling dogs, the sweet-sour smell of cooking spices, the admiring glances of three dusky schoolgirls. A
swaddled baby lies in a doorway, but he doesn't cry.

It's unclean, seething, confused. Yet there's no hint of India's
squalid poverty. These people laugh, flirt, and walk with pride.
They may have no money, but their stomachs are miraculously
full, and for six days I have not heard a voice raised in anger.
But Karim is impatient with my soliloquy.

He dislikes Sukarno intensely ("that old he-goat") and wants
me to see the supreme "masterpiece," so we cruise past the ex-
president's grandiose and very empty Senajan Stadium, once
planned as the Orient's incomparable showcase. It's vast, preten-
tious, and brutally concrete. And how many does it seat? "Maybe
100,000, 150,000? Who cares?" says Karim. "It's no bloody
use to anybody now." So with an impulsive snort, he decides
to show me Djakarta's other oddities, such as the Ministry of
Religion, the Chinese Embassy, and Tanjung Priok.

The Ministry of Religion is a unique and decidedly surrealist
affair. From its five air-conditioned floors, some three thousand
imams, bonzes, and priests bravely try to keep the lid on Indonesia's theological powder keg. They untangle the unending
hassles between Muslims, Buddhists, Hindus, Christians, ani-
mists, and vaguer cults. They dictate the number of national religious holidays, which is a headache; how many wives are per-
missible; whether a god can live in a banyan; whether the witch
doctors should be registered. "If you don't have a religion,"
Karim explains dryly, "the government says you're a Communist. Therefore the best bet, these days, is to have five religions
. . . and maybe five wives."

Actually, Karim is only half joking, for the Ministry of Religion is Suharto's pet brainchild, and just ten minutes later, we
see grim proof that the Generals don't take Communism lightly.
Behind heavy wooden gates, now firmly padlocked, the once all-
powerful embassy of Red China stands burned and gutted, a

smoke-blackened, deserted ruin. Karim draws two fingers across his neck and smiles darkly.

Yet despite the massacres, 500,000 Chinese still uneasily co-exist in the capital, and as we drive north towards the sea, the coppery profiles grow paler, the eyes noticeably more pinched. We've reached Tanjung Priok, Djakarta's Chinatown, the water-front swamp where the Dutch first settled.

Down a shaded side street, we find a dilapidated but charming red brick home with diamond-pane casements, a sloping, tiled roof, and a clock tower. The house might have been plucked from a Vermeer, and behind a banner scrawled with Chinese callig-raphy, there's the telltale plaque: "Anno 1629."

During the seventeenth century, this flourishing seaport ri-valed Bombay and Shanghai. But nowadays, moon-faced Canton-ese have squatters' rights in the old Flemish mansions, living ten to a room, hanging the washing from the windows. Their pigtailed children, in flowered pajamas, romp across the canal bridges; the solid Dutch warehouses are abandoned; rows of tightly packed booths sell noodles and dried seaweed. Crouched on their haunches, Chinese grannies haggle over the price of two needles or a box of matches, and Karim, who feels out of place, says cruelly: "In Chinatown you can buy anything from a lemon to a twelve-year-old girl."

Irritably, Karim pulls my sleeve and draws me away from the noisy crowds, across a causeway, and into a derelict, moss-grown fort. He kicks one of its ancient brass cannons, leaps nimbly up the watchtower's steps. Suddenly it's very still, and below us, a brackish canal thick with gulfweed runs to the ocean. In the year 1596, the first Dutch frigate sent its musketeers down these waters. "This is where all our troubles began," Karim says bit-terly. "It took us 350 years to get rid of the bastards!"

3 As dusk falls, both the temper and climate of Djakarta cool down. The dust settles, the smoke-spewing buses vanish, tumult turns into tranquillity. Aimlessly we drift toward the great, sprawling market place known as Senen, where sparks from a thousand fires flicker into the night. Like

Marrakesh's Djema el Fnaa, it's a spectacle staged by De Mille.
Acrobats tumble, jugglers toss flaming torches, and a loin-clothed skeleton is eating light bulbs. Another mystic is frying eggs on his head. Clowns with paint-streaked faces joke obscenely, gray-bearded storytellers spellbind their circles of wide-eyed children, while medicine men wrapped in orange turbans offer potions for every ill from tired blood to broken hearts. "Hold on to your watch," says Karim. "Our pickpockets have clever fingers."

The eddying throng moves quietly and without haste. There is no jostling. The bare feet pick their way unerringly between the trays of vanilla and sandalwood powder. Cross-legged on open blankets, the tradesmen ignore their clients, squatting impassively between heaps of coffee beans, garlic, and tight bunches of peanuts, between grunting stacks of palm-cord baskets with pigs inside, between bolts of cloth, singing birds, plump pineapples, caged fireflies, and cobras. Over glowing braziers, old crones hunch like witches, frying bananas and sweet yams, and overall, there hangs an indefinable, aromatic cloud. It's the smell of cloves, which Indonesians blend with their tobacco.

The midnight air is mellow, and Karim's eyes are roving as he admires the slim, undulating contours of Java's women, voluptuous yet modest in their ankle-length *kain*. "Our girls ripen early," he smiles, "as do our fruits." And without explanation, Karim spins on his heels, walks a block or two, then turns down a narrow, dimly lit alley. We sneak past a police box with a drowsing sergeant, and Karim's friends wink. Behind iron-barred windows, there's the unmistakable outline of a bed and naked female shadows.

We're in the quarter called Little Paris, and evidently here's one problem which Suharto's puritans have *not* solved. From a doorway, a scrawny arm strikes out and clutches my shoulder. She's about thirteen, rumpled, and chewing betel nut. Karim thrusts her away. "Let's beat it," he says abruptly. "People get knifed down here." So we go to eat instead.

Djakarta's night life, as can be seen, is hardly exhilarating. Being a strait-laced Muslim city, there are neither clubs nor bars, and the social whirl means ginger pop at a roadside stall. Yet Karim promises a final ace. So after dinner, we hail two passing *betjak* and get pedaled to the People's Entertainment Park, which despite its sterile name is pretty extraordinary.

For a start, this gamy collection of side shows has been set down in dead-center, midtown Djakarta, right next to Sukarno's National Monument. Like opening a burlesque show opposite the Lincoln Memorial. And as we enter, a steel-helmeted riot cop frisks my pockets, then curtly prods me inside with his submachine gun.

The People's Park somehow combines all the more lunatic qualities of contemporary Indonesia. Down a one-time triumphal avenue, Beatle-mopped teenagers now race their go-karts. Like berserk kamikaze, they jump the sidewalks, screech between the palms, chase down a walking victim, or play suicidal "chicken," while across the way, a twenty-five-piece gamelan rings its gongs for half-empty benches. On the left we pass an open-air go-go joint. The wild kids jerk with epileptic abandon, and the barker promises: "Don't worry about partners! We'll look after you!" Next door there's a birth control clinic. And a slot machine for condoms.

In a bamboo shanty, we find the casino. It's run by Djakarta's military governor. The top stake is twenty-five cents. A painted sign reads "Check All Knives and Pistols at the Desk." And two unsmiling MPs slouch at the door with bayonets fixed. The casino is flanked by the Baptist Mission. We stroll past a row of foul-smelling booths, where they're hawking fly-covered hunks of mutton and other delicacies. Behind, a billboard states simply "Entero-Vioform Is Best."

There's also a shooting gallery with apparently live ammunition, an insistent minority of pimps, hustlers peddling pot, and inside one creaking pavilion, an absolutely ravishing team of dancing girls. Their mascaraed eyes flash; lustrous, raven hair flows down their slender shoulders. Perfumed and provocative, they roll their hips and shamelessly ogle the customers. Karim laughs. "There's only one drawback," he says. "They're all men. Djakarta is full of sister boys." I decide it's high time to go home.

In Indonesia, things are seldom what they first seem, and this can prove repeatedly unnerving. So back at the hotel, I drop in for a nightcap, and as at all times, the bar is packed. Germans, French, English, Americans—they're drinking with the tenacity of despair. Disgruntled, cranky, they're businessmen who came to do business and, in most cases, didn't. And their frustrations seem as endless as they are repetitive.

"Nothing changes in this dump, mate. Except these days the Army gets *all* the ruddy cumshaw!"

"Christ! I chased a shipment of quinine for three months and finally discovered it didn't even exist."

"Two bloody cops hijacked my car, and it's now being driven by a major in Bandung."

"Those f——g Generals! I've hosted fifteen dinners and still have no contract."

"Money has no meaning in Indonesia. They barter cassava for coconuts. That's all they understand."

"The troops broke into the hotel kitchen again tonight."

"These blasted people don't even know what time means."

It's the other side of the coin, and by their own values, the foreigners are, of course, right. For time and tensions don't exist in Indonesia. And payola is a way of life. Clocks, even calendars, are purely decorative. Like promises, they serve no useful purpose. So after squandering a week, I capitulate, as one frequently does in this country. I tear up my tidy, ten-page schedule, forget both my general and his car, and catch the overnight train to Jogjakarta.

■4■ Most Indonesian railways might have been resurrected from D. W. Griffith's *The Great Train Robbery*. The engines have cowcatchers and bulbous smokestacks, and the grimy, wooden carriages look like shantytown on wheels. But the prestigious Bima, which rattles down Java's backbone from the capital to Surabaya, is Indonesia's first and only "express," which means it can, when lucky, hit a respectable fifty miles per hour. Custom-built in the People's Republic of East Germany, the Bima is diesel-fired, has flush toilets. It also has bunks for sleeping and an air-conditioning plant which can't decide between igloo-icy and steambath-torrid. But I can't complain. On my trip we had only three nonscheduled stops. Twice for errant buffalo and once for an old lady asleep on the tracks.

And as we slowly draw out of Djakarta, nudging goats and roosters to safety, small children run up waving and throwing flowers. Picking up speed, we roll past the nation's most blighted slums, tactfully shrouded in bougainvillaea. Minute by minute, the hot, dusty, urban disorder thins out, dissolves.

Then suddenly, extravagantly, on every side, the countryside of Java explodes in all its green, green, matchless opulence. The contrast is breath-catching, almost shocking, a stunning coup de théâtre. The green rice shoots sweep from horizon to horizon, gently rippling in the breeze, with green-drenched hamlets marooned like islands between the paddies. Majestic coco palms, forests of bananas, green thickets of bamboo. A luxuriance of mangoes, papayas, and breadfruit, cotton, tea, rubber, oil and sago palms, and everywhere the clear, sparkling streams of life-kindling water.

It's a scene so immodestly prodigal that it makes Tahiti look barren. It's the lush fertility of the jungle that has been tamed and put to use. Caressed by sunshine and monsoon rains, the soil is so rich that maize yields in seven weeks and a banana tree grows in ten. It's no wonder Indonesians don't know hunger. Yet mile after mile, the flooded paddies just mirror the clouds, uncared for by toiling peasants. Once in a while we pass naked boys with coolie hats crouched motionless across a buffalo's haunches, but otherwise the land is deserted. In Indonesia, men do the planting and reaping, but Nature is the best husbandman. She bountifully provides two, even three, rice crops a year. And I thought of India, where every grain must be coaxed with tragic concern.

Empty dreams, squandered billions. Djakarta's vainglorious National ▶
Monument, built by deposed President Sukarno, pokes forlornly into a
cheerless sky. It's the capital's mightiest monument, and its flaming tip is
gilded with twenty-four-carat pure gold. But most people couldn't care less.
Tending a rickety food stall, these three women have more serious matters to
discuss. Like the spiraling cost of dog meat.

But Senator W., who's sharing my dining-car table, offers the inevitable enigma, Indonesian style. Senator W., who is forty and a former colonel, has ten children and earns thirty dollars a month. He's also a hard-pressed member of the Budget Committee. "Rice!" he grunts. *"Of course* we have enough rice. That's why we're importing 600,000 tons this year!" Senator W. scoops up another curried mouthful with his fingers. "The government offers the peasants $75 a ton, but the Chinese merchants offer $100. So the peasants sell to the Chinese, who smuggle the rice to Singapore. Then the government buys back the same rice at $200 a ton!" But, good grief, why not just pay the peasants more? The honorable Senator looks at me as if I'm demented. "But we don't have enough money to buy *all* the rice!"

I'm no economist, but the senator's Kafkaesque plight gives me another sleepless night, and when at a grisly 3 A.M. the Bima lurches into Jogjakarta, I'm still cockeyed. At times, Indonesia requires a cooler head than mine. And anyway, I appear to have arrived at an outpost in mid-Sahara.

Outside the station, half a dozen faceless Tuareg muffled in flowing burnooses crouch silently around a dying bonfire. No welcoming "salaam" tonight. There's a cluster of palms and nothing else, so I sit on my suitcase, and an hour or so later, an ancient jeep clatters out of the shadows. "Goodnight," says the driver. "I've been waiting for you. Yesterday I'll show you everything." I decide to call it a day.

■**5**■ Jogjakarta is Java's Kyoto. "We're slow-motion people," says my guide, Ariesta. "We walk slowly, live slowly, and change slowly." For centuries past, Jogjakarta has been the sanctuary of artists and craftsmen,

◀ *On a bleak sidewalk facing Djakarta's first and only expressway, two enterprising, off-duty soldiers have set up an impromptu gas station. Their wares have been discreetly filched from military depots and sell at bargain prices. As a backdrop, empty steel skeletons rise dejectedly from deserted building sites. The grandiose projects, initiated by Sukarno, have been shelved. Forever.*

writers and philosophers; and even today, this calm, leisurely city takes a slightly snobbish pride in being Java's historic and cultural capital. Its citizens hold singing contests for birds and create the most delicate silver filigree; they breed peacocks and lovingly stage the longest, most sumptuous temple dances. Djakarta, it's conceded, is a boorish catastrophe.

While Attila the Hun was sacking Europe, the sultans of Jogjakarta were already trading silks with distant Cathay and dispatching scholars to Benares. And as early as the eighth and ninth centuries, the ruling dynasties were renowned across the Orient for their refined and civilized ways, for their jeweled pleasure domes, for the epic splendors of Borobudur and the Prambanan temples.

Eleven centuries later, both the monuments and the mood survive. As a modern university town, Jogja perpetuates its traditions of scholarship, while its painters, sculptors, and artisans are Indonesia's elite. Like Kyoto's people, they are proud but not patronizing. They simply *know* they're better, so they can afford to be affable.

After the turmoil of Djakarta, this tranquil, orderly city is refreshing. The trim, tree-lined avenues swarm with student cyclists and fringe-topped pony carts; yet at night there's the heady scent of frangipani and a medieval hush. Even Suharto's paratroopers seem slightly awed. They keep to the back streets, shuffling uneasily. Like country boys with plastic popguns.

Within the Republic of Indonesia, aristocratic Jogjakarta enjoys special status. Although Sukarno liquidated the nobility and grabbed their estates, Jogja has both a reigning sultan, Hamengku Buwono IX, and a fully staffed palace, the Kraton. "The sultan has *mystery*," says Ariesta. "What you would call occult power. Unlike the other rajas, he fought the Dutch like a lion. He never lost a battle. That's why Sukarno spared him. When the sultan passes, we fall on our knees and worship." Whatever his psychic prowess, Sultan Hamengku Buwono is a gifted economist and doubles as Indonesia's minister of economic affairs. He's also got four concubines and thirty-two children. Yet so far he's refused to take a queen. The sultan wants to terminate the dynasty once and for all, and he can't risk spawning an heir. "The sultan is very democratic," says Ariesta.

His Royal Highness is out of town, however, presumably untangling the nation's chaotic finances; so we visit his palace instead. In the hot sunshine, we stroll past flaking, whitewashed ramparts smothered in wisteria and tangled hibiscus, past two senescent guards with glazed eyes and enormous lances, and ("Goodness gracious!" as Anna would have said) we've stumbled right into a studio set for *The King and I*. Devised in the mid-eighteenth century, the Kraton might be a fantasy by Beaton. Airy, theatrical, amusing—one hundred wonderful acres of potted plants and Far East rococo.

Between raked-earth courtyards, a dozen gilded pavilions, their tiled roofs raised on slender columns, stand open and windowless. Naturally there are neither walls nor doors. Like Chinese temples, the roofs hang rather than slope, bowing under an excess of corkscrew dragons and other curlicued trivia. The floors are marbled or blindingly ceramic, Persian rugs lie randomly scattered, the low teak couches are elaborately carved. In one pavilion, the sultan's private gamelan slumbers through its weekly rehearsal. In another, loyal retainers are playing cribbage.

Shaded by a monstrous, knotted banyan, we find the sultan's mosque and the sultan's observatory, a shrine for his magic-endowed kris, and an outhouse filled with gold-tasseled but unused palanquins. Potted ferns and potted orchids, fussy friezes and brocaded screens, and wherever there's space, the endearing bric-a-brac of provincial royalty—a plaster-of-paris Venus, broken grandfather clocks, Victorian gas lamps, and tinkling chandeliers from Murano.

As we move away, a gong sounds. Under a turquoise parasol five court ladies trip solemnly across the courtyard. The eldest carries a silver tray with a Chinese teapot and cups. "They will prepare tea for the sultan," says Ariesta. "They do this twice every day, even if he's not here. It's the custom."

As it is, traditions die hard in Jogja, and even Sultan Hamengku Buwono IX is not immune. Once a year he ritually cuts his hair, fingernails, and toenails, bundles together his old clothes, then makes the seventeen-mile pilgrimage to the big sand dunes at Parangtritis. Here the disciple of Keynes and Galbraith dutifully throws hair, nail clippings, and clothes into the the ocean. This devotion, it's said, helps placate the sea spirits. Maybe even the World Bank.

■6■ Sapto the Painter is a celebrity. He owns both a Mercedes and a Vespa. He's rich, recognized, and has the urbane good looks of Claude Dauphin. His full name is Saptohudojo, and he's probably Indonesia's best, most adventurous painter. In a land where silence is usually safer, Sapto is also disarmingly outspoken. "In the old days, Sukarno's ministers came here," he says. "Now Suharto's come." And he smiles.

Sapto lives and works in Jogja by choice. He owns a cozy thatched home with bamboo-plaited walls and a fishpond in the living room. He makes his own paints, fires pottery in the incinerator, scours the scrap market for materials—milk cans, cycle chains, and rusting bolts, seashells, sand, and driftwood. Anything goes. Isolation has forced Sapto to improvise, which he enjoys, and his tactile, flamboyant collages reflect this pleasure. They're as witty as a 3-D Braque, as upbeat as Sapto himself.

In his early twenties, he impulsively quit Indonesia and hitchhiked to London. Via Penang, Kabul, Isfahan, and without a nickel. He paid his way with folk songs and impromptu shadow plays. "I had a broken heart, so I fled," he says wryly. "Then in Singapore I met Kartika. She was fourteen. I proposed. Her father said maybe. So I went on my way. Two years later, we met by chance in Hyde Park, and her father changed his mind. We were married the next morning." Yet after just four years, the inane complexities of Western life drove them home to Jogja.

Talking softly, thoughtfully, Sapto explains that Europe does not have the harmony of Indonesia. "You may think us anarchic, superstitious, even childish," he says, "yet we have cohesion and continuity." Whatever Djakarta does, the inbred peasant qualities of patience, tolerance, and resigned common sense endure. Despite poverty, corruption, and other afflictions, adds Sapto, there's an invisible framework that allows Indonesia's people to survive—an unspoken, yet universal, convention under which art, religion, and daily life become inseparable yet interchangeable.

A village festival is both a religious *and* an artistic occasion; a peasant may be a fine sculptor and vice versa. A farmer will exorcise the demons in his paddy, then pray in the mosque; a laborer will dig ditches for three weeks, then impetuously carve a bust of Vishnu. Probably for his Buddhist employer. "You've seen them making batik," says Sapto. "One cloth may need six months. But are these old women artists or artisans? I think they're both. And this gives them pride."

This indulgent dualism allows a muezzin to be a moneylender and a farm girl to be a dazzling *legong* dancer. It also permits people to turn a cremation into a jamboree, to persecute Chinese merchants when pressed for cash, simultaneously to fear and love Indonesia's ubiquitous spirits. For an outsider, it's a confusing, alien concept, and Sapto notices my puzzlement. "Come," he says. "I'll show you."

For half an hour we drive into the rich countryside, past terraced rice paddies, bouncing down a rutted lane under a green vault of bamboo until we reach a river. On foot we cross a narrow, slatted bridge, which sways perilously, then climb the hill into Kasongan, the potters' village.

No radio, no school, no electricity. Just two dozen huts tucked away in the bamboo forest. Mothers suckling their infants, gray pigs with low-slung bellies, and the squawk of parakeets. And on every porch, the young girls spinning their potter's wheels with nimble feet, while deftly throwing the clay with their hands—calmly, tenderly, with an artist's concern.

We meet the village chief. He's fat, brown, and cheerful. He wears a batik sarong knotted at the waist. The chief introduces his wife. She's fourteen and pregnant. "The village has had troubles," he says. The Army sent a sergeant. "Make more pots," ordered the sergeant. But the villagers ignored him. The sergeant grew angry. But still the villagers would not talk. After eight weeks, the sergeant went away. The chief is clearly delighted.

In the dappled sunshine, plump, naked babies totter happily between the goats and chickens, while a slender beauty scatters camellia petals before a small, stone shrine. This will keep the devils away tonight. Across the way, an old man chisels at a block of wood. He's almost completed an excitingly stylized tiger and I offer to buy. "No, not yet," he says doubtfully. "But next week, maybe . . ."

In every yard, the damp, lustrous pots stand drying in the sun. Tomorrow they will be fired with blazing straw. Then they will be carried ten miles to market, where they will be sold for seven cents each. It's primitive and laborious, yet the busy girls chatter and laugh, smiling shyly as we pass. As dusk falls, the villagers gather and walk two miles to the mosque.

"What is civilization?" asks Sapto. "Isn't it maybe the chance to be happy on your own terms? These people have a rhythm to their life. They're part and parcel of our landscape and our history. Like Borobudur. It's not simply a monument. Once upon a time, I used to visit Borobudur every day. It became part of me, part of my work. I know every single stone."

■**7**■ I met my first general at Borobudur. Watched by giggling children, poised on tiptoe, he had an arm thrust through a stone lattice and was groping wildly. For a general, it was a distinctly undignified position. Yet he awkwardly persisted, and after ten frantic minutes, his perspiring face beamed with triumph. The general had touched the fingers of the hidden Buddha, and according to legend, this would bring everlasting good fortune. "You see," said Ariesta, "even our generals need Borobudur."

The Hindu temples at Prambanan may be more refined, more delicate in design and detail, but Borobudur is Indonesia's greatest monument. Like the Pyramids or Stonehenge, it's everyone's reminder that life goes on, as well as being the biggest Buddhist temple in all Southeast Asia.

This mighty stone heap, shaped like a gigantic stupa (the bell shape which is Buddhism's most primitive form), may lack the jungled mystery of Angkor Wat or the elegant symmetry of the Taj, yet it's built on the same prodigious scale, and Ariesta recites his lesson with pride. Two million cubic feet of stone, three miles of bas-relief friezes, ten terraces, 504 statues of the Buddha. And as happens in Indonesia, the whole business will collapse in a decade, unless President Suharto can raise three million dollars for repairs.

Between purple mountains, the mossy, charcoal mass of Borobudur sprawls solid, inert, and remote. From a distance, it has a permanence, simplicity, and earthy magnificence that is primeval. It's awesome rather than beautiful, a geometric progression rather than a masterpiece. There's no entrance, no exit, no roof, no altar, and nowhere to sit. It's all superlatively illogical and impractical. Like Everest, Borobudur is simply *there*.

Under the patronage of the Sailendra dynasty, the Medici of Central Java, the mammoth pile was completed about A.D. 850. It took ten thousand workers and one hundred years to build. Defaced by Muslim vandals, Borobudur sprouted weeds and slid into oblivion until 1814, when it was rediscovered by an Englishman, Sir Stamford Raffles, whose forces briefly held Java during the Napoleonic Wars.

Borobudur was initially planned as a sanctuary for Buddhist monks and pilgrims, a refuge where they could meditate and plot their course towards Nirvana. But today is Sunday and the monument is fairly crawling with visitors. Schoolboys play hide-and-seek between the five hundred smaller stupas, the general takes snaps of his wife in Pucci blouse and stretch pants.

Yet as we climb the steep, high steps ("The way to heaven is never easy"), the crowds dissolve and a breeze whistles between the fissures. From their niches, the stone Buddhas half smile, yet each statue has its distinct pose and expression ("Truth has a million faces"); and on every side, the intricate friezes unfold like medieval tapestries, endlessly extolling the infinite benevolence of the Buddha.

On the final terrace, where "thoughts are no longer tied to earth," a shaven bonze paces the narrow walk, mumbling his sutras, a mongrel dog sleeps, and three sparrows admire the view. The dome of the crowning stupa once held a half-finished Buddha ("The unfinished Buddha inside us all"), but it's long gone. And somehow it doesn't matter. It's quiet here and inexplicably serene.

Between black thunderclouds, steely shafts of sunlight strike the palms below, playing lazily across the ponderous pile of Borobudur, across the multiple stupas arrayed like sentinels, across an immensity of plinths and platforms. Repetitive, monotonous, yet curiously hypnotic. You feel safe. And unlike Machu Picchu or the Mayan temples of Yucatan, Borobudur is innocent. Human blood has never been spilled on these terraces. Maybe that is the charisma.

■8■ *"Just* down the road," said Ariesta, "and the best in Java." Distance, like time, is a disposable item in Indonesia, so we've just driven sixty miles or more just to catch a theater show in Solo. Our *wayang wong* play, which is just a brief excerpt from the Hindu *Mahabharata*, will end at 2 A.M. after just six hours. Front row center, we now sprawl in rattan chairs, and a cat is licking my toes. I can't understand a word, but I'm enjoying myself hugely.

Show business in Solo, it should be noted, has little in common with Broadway. The renowned Sriwedari Theater might be a converted airplane hangar. It has a corrugated iron roof, cracked walls, and wire netting in the windows. The best tickets cost sixty cents and the cheapest ten; and tonight, as every night, all 1,500 seats are filled. S.R.O., and the repertoire hasn't changed since anyone can remember. But who cares? It's easier that way.

Across the way, the idling gamelan players pick their teeth, scratch, and chitchat, while their girl singer knits. Squatting cross-legged, eyes half closed, they strike their gongs with the drowsiest nonchalance, stretch out to pluck a two-stringed *rabab* or pick up a half-forgotten flute. It's anarchy in action, yet music somehow happens. "Our players have *pada rasakake*," says Ariesta. "They feel with each other." They also know every discordant note by heart and punctuate every stage action with uncanny, unfailing precision. No score, no melody, no beat. Yet the sounds are mellow, complex, and impalpably languid. Shades of the MJQ.

Next to me, a colonel and his regal grandmother have brought three babies and seven other children. The infants spasmodically howl, and the colonel, despite his Sandhurst mustache, has taken off his shoes. Down the aisles, barefoot boys are loudly hawking soda pop and peanuts.

It's casual, noisy, and participatory, like Elizabethan theater. You meet your friends, change places, smoke, and it lasts forever. Yet it's also exciting. On stage, *wayang wong* blends the improvised brilliance of commedia dell'arte with circus horseplay and the hidden tensions of ballet. Like most things Indonesian, it's a paradox.

As always, the script opens in Heaven and ends in Heaven. On assignment from Vishnu, the god Shiva descends to earth, resolves various mortal dilemmas, then flies home. During the intervening six hours and forty-nine scenes, however, anything goes. The wilder, the weirder, the better.

Shiva, who is played by a woman, gets pinched by the clowns, seduced by a lesbian, and half raped by a forest demon, attacked by pirates, swept away by a typhoon, and swallowed by a volcano. The grotesquely painted clowns fling cream pies, tout cough medicine, mime a volleyball game, teach Shiva how to play poker, and stick out their tongues at the audience. And between the solemn speeches, there's a maelstrom of sword fighting, magic, and juggling, bawdy jokes, and split-second *pentjak*, Java's particularly vicious form of karate.

It's a madcap formula. Jumbled, irrational, even sacrilegious. Yet it works. *Wayang wong*, say some, allows the people to blow off steam, for the play reflects the country's deepest conflict, everyman's tug-of-war between passion and self-control. Which possibly explains tonight's most extraordinary touch, the behavior of Shiva.

Despite the ribaldry and the slapstick, the actress sticks to the centuries-old conventions and keeps her ritual cool. When she fights, she strikes like a cobra. When she speaks, even her cheek muscles don't flinch. It's the final exercise in mind over body and amazing to watch. On one occasion, while being insufferably taunted by the clowns, she does not flicker an eyelash for fully forty minutes. She stands tense yet motionless. Then when the morons leave, her fingers tremble and she begins to dance. She holds the stage alone for the next hour.

Actually, Widjajati does not dance. She glides. Her bare feet hardly stroke the ground. In her tightly bound sarong, flecked with gold, she moves from the hips. Slowly, softly, tenderly. Her tapered fingers flutter, her huge brown eyes smolder; yet the beautiful, fine-boned face hides all emotion. She flicks her pink sash, deftly kicks her train; yet her golden neck and shoulders are without life. Her breathing is invisible, as are her muscles. Widjajati has been training since she was five.

"Impossibly decelerated grace," it's been said. "Every gesture defies anatomy and gravity." Whatever the tricks, it's superb. Widjajati is like liquid gold in motion. She moves in a trance, yet her radiations are unmistakably feline, sensual, almost erotic. And the excitement is apparently catching.

"I shall go to visit my fiancée tonight," Ariesta says casually. "I cycle eight miles twice a week to see her. She's also a dancer." Back at the hotel, I offer Ariesta my taxi, but bowing politely, he refuses. "Oh, no," he says, "that would be different. I must cycle. It's the custom."

■**9**■ In Indonesia, you don't travel, you improvise movements. From Jogja, the road swings northeast to Surabaya, but the buses are booked solid for three weeks. So I hire a cab instead. My driver is a college lecturer who teaches chemistry and charges me double. Like all Indonesians, he's moonlighting. He also seems to confuse highway travel with a bullfight on wheels.

Hand on horn, Chipto hurtles through the world's worst traffic with an assurance that is terrifying. We squeeze crazily between groaning trucks and smoking buses, zigzag through swarms of *betjak*, horse buggies, and oxcarts, haphazardly scattering geese and cyclists, chickens and strolling peasants. On screeching tires, we happen to be charging through the most thickly populated area on earth, but Chipto is not impressed. And promptly ignores the only traffic light east of Djakarta.

Chipto's foot is glued to the pedal. It's neither the time nor the place for sightseeing. Still, I do have fleeting, white-knuckled memories of the twin volcanoes known as Merapi and Merabu, teak forests, big red banners which scream "Down with Moral Decadence!", rustling acres of sugar cane and tobacco, and the ubiquitous jigsaw of rice paddies. Then in mid-afternoon, we hit the monsoon.

Within minutes, the dikes erupt. The rain squall hits our roof like machine-gun fire. A torrential river pours across the road. Visibility is zero, but Chipto keeps his foot on the gas. Skidding and sliding, plowing through clouds of spray, we dodge eerie phantom shapes, knock something or somebody into a ditch, and after ten hours and just 170 miles, reach Surabaya. Will I need him tomorrow? asks Chipto. I smile wanly and call for a beer. A big one, please.

Three hours later, I'm with Tjiptono. He's Chinese, twenty-six, married, and vivaciously charming. We're eating in the open air. Wood benches, dirt floor, and cats howling at every table leg. It's hot, hot, hot in Surabaya. Maybe 105 or more. We're drenched with sweat, and I've just mistakenly swallowed a chili that makes Tabasco taste like tomato juice. We're nibbling through a selection of *sate*, tiny cubes of chicken and lamb that get skewered, barbecued, and dunked in a peppery peanut sauce. There's also a dish of sheep's eyes that keeps looking my way. Still, the *sate* is delicious.

"Me doctor. Earn three dollars one month. Most people no pay," says Tjiptono. "But me also sell 217 article last eighteen month, and that make me plenty rich!" He laughs. "Now get top rate. One dollar for story." Unlike Chipto, friend Tjiptono has *seven* jobs. He's a practicing physician, aide to the governor, tourist guide, magazine writer, shipping clerk, AP stringer, and occasional chauffeur. He's also staggeringly enthusiastic.

Would I like to see the Heroes' Monument, which looks like Asia's biggest ballpoint pen? Would I care to visit the zoo where the crocodiles come from Surabaya's backwaters and the giant *komodo* dragon eats four dogs for breakfast? Would I like to see the Soviet-built cruiser, which hasn't put to sea for three years? Would I care to view the bull races on nearby Madura, where the yoked steers cover a hundred meters in nine seconds? Wouldn't I like to visit Surabaya's six department stores, where, despite all Indonesia's money crises, you can buy everything from rubber falsies to Levis, plastic hibiscus, "Miss Dior," and postcards of Betty Grable?

Eventually, as happens in Indonesia, I was shown everything except what I wanted to see, which was the bulls. But tonight I'm stubborn. I want to see *kuda kepang*, East Java's notorious "horse trance." I'd watched a shoddy imitation in Jogja, which cost me twenty dollars and was a phony. I was both disenchanted and skeptical, but Tjiptono shrugs his shoulders. "Jogja people topside no savvy," he says. "Now we go People's Park. You look-see."

The poetry of Java. Color, calm, and time for thought. ABOVE: *In the hush of dawn, a lonely, barefoot peddler pads through a drowsing, mist-hung village in the highlands. Chanting a mournful cry, the hawker hopes to unload his two baskets of avocados before the market opens. If he's weary or wretched, he'll probably blow the profits on a fistful of hash.* BELOW: *Caught in the privacy of their garden, two young ladies and a thoughtful chaperone exchange confidences. Like Jane Austen heroines, these Jogjakarta girls shelter under a parasol, talk softly, dreamily, respecting the niceties. They're both poised and gracious, and as they chitchat, their mouths form the quizzical half smile that their suitors find so seductive. Unlike the peddler, they never smoke pot.*

OVERLEAF: *Prambanan is all delicacy. Unlike massive, sprawling Borobudur, these ancient Hindu temples are masterpieces of elegant symmetry, as refined and civilized as the mighty Sailendra dynasty that devised them. They were begun in the ninth century and completed in the tenth. Set in a lush, sweeping valley outside Jogjakarta, Prambanan still welcomes hermits and holy men and once a year is the scene of the sumptuous* Ramayana *dance festival. It's maybe worth noting that militant Islam, which has been around since the thirteenth century, has left no comparable aesthetic imprint.*

■**10**■ Like a voodoo rite in Haiti, *kuda kepang* opens with deceptive calm. On a wide, wooden stage, the crouched musicians strike up a slow, persistent beat: two drums, two gongs, a flute, and a man who beats a steel pipe with a hammer. *One-two one-two one-two.* Four dancers riding black bamboo hobbyhorses begin circling each other. They dip and turn clumsily, jogging from side to side. *One-two one-two.* The dancers are scrawny, ragged, and have walked eighty miles from their village. They're short of cash.

Ten minutes, twenty minutes. Then imperceptibly the rhythm gets faster, louder, more insistent. The dancers start to canter and strike each other with whips. *Two-one two-one.* The dancers break into a gallop. Their faces glisten. They pant, grit their teeth, draw away, then charge. Again and again. The tom-toms pound. My ears throb. The stage is shaking. *Two-one two-one.* They're slashing each other's faces. Blood trickles. Then, suddenly, one dancer pitches on his face.

Two men rush out, pick him up, place the hobbyhorse between his legs. His muscles are taut as steel and his eyes stare vacantly. He begins to dance. Stiffly, awkwardly, like a puppet. "He's in trance," says Tjiptono. "He thinks he's horse." And by now so do his partners. They prance and whinny, toss their heads, stamp their hooves. One dancer drops on his knees, thrusts his head into a pail, and slobbers the water. The others get a fistful of grass, which they chew and swallow.

From the wings, the *dukun* watches anxiously. Before the show, he burned incense and called the spirits. He's both witch

"Love, like youth, is wasted on the young." Maybe. But not in Indonesia. Most children reach puberty before eleven. Like the fruit, they ripen early. And by the age of thirteen or less, there are few secrets left. ABOVE: *With twinkling fingers, two exquisite young* legong *dancers trace the delicate arabesques of* oleg tambulilingan, *a highly explicit caper between two bumblebees. The girls began dancing when they were five. They are now fourteen, and their mothers are frantic because they're still not married.* BELOW: *Squatting on their haunches, three boys busily scoop up sweet, sticky rice from banana-leaf plates. Their sisters are home scrubbing floors and washing clothes. These young boys have learned their rights quickly. In Indonesia, it's the women who do the work.*

doctor, medium, and impresario. Kneeling down, the *dukun* clicks his fingers and one dancer grovels towards him. The man's mouth is foaming; his eyes are fearful, pleading. It's barbaric, horrible, and shamefully exciting. But the show's only started.

The *dukun* gestures impatiently and three aides seize the dancer, wrench open his clenched hands, and tear away the hobbyhorse. They place a heavy dragon's mask over his head, then unleash him. The cringing Amhal is transformed. Screaming and shaking, yet still dancing, he drops his head and savagely attacks his comrades. *Two-one two-one.* The gongs crash, hypnotic and unforgiving. *Two-one two-one.* Like raging anvils. The dancers circle Amhal, flailing him viciously. The dragon's wooden teeth open and snap shut. A dancer shrieks, and I'm getting scared.

We're sitting on stage, which is too close for comfort. On which Tjiptono foolishly explodes a flashbulb into the dragon's face. The half-crazed Amhal charges. He knocks Tjiptono to the ground, then butts him fiercely and repeatedly. Amhal turns, sees me, rushes, and hits me in the ribs. He topples me clear off the stage.

I climb back and the *dukun* looks panicky. The show's got out of hand. It's pandemonium. The mesmerized "horses" are still jogging, but Amhal is fighting like a wildcat. He's using his mask for a war club. His comrades crumple, then rise dazedly. One dancer sways offstage, tumbles down fifteen stairs, and stays spread-eagled. The *dukun* dashes down. He presses the dancer's temples, pushes thumbs into his eyes, blows into his ears. The man breathes heavily, shakes his head, and wakes. He doesn't remember a thing.

The *dukun* bolts back on stage. His aides grab one dancer at a time, subdue him, and the witch doctor breaks his spell. One dancer is carried off stiff as a corpse. Another is pinned to the floor for five minutes and keeps screaming, "I want to dance! I want to dance!" The *dukun* slaps him roughly and he recovers. But the dragon has gone berserk.

Amhal chases his own shadow across the stage, bounding and screeching like a banshee. He chops down three aides, mauls a third. In a tight half-circle, the *dukun* and his men finally drive

Amhal towards the backstage door. The dragon pitches head first down the steep stairs and collapses. Five men grasp his arms and legs. Amhal begins to twitch and tremble. His eyes quiver like a madman's.

The *dukun* throws water over him, punches his face, then whispers in his ear. A *mantra*, a call to the demon within. "Come out! Come out!" he says. "No! No! The devil says no!" shrieks Amhal. "Come out! Come out!" "No! No! No!" Amhal's whole body shakes spasmodically. Then, ever so slowly, his eyes open. They flicker briefly. "Who am I?" he asks weakly. And passes out. Amhal, who makes ten cents a show, has been in trance seven times tonight.

■11■ *Kuda kepang* is repellent, degrading, and absolutely enthralling. It's the other side of the coin. Unlike the delicate Widjajati, Amhal freaks out. It's body over mind. The darker shores of Indonesia. *Kuda kepang*, which plays with the stuff of madness, is also a dangerous game. Its dancers die young and often insane. Tjiptono, who has studied the phenomenon, claims the *dukun* uses neither drugs, alcohol, nor hypnosis. The doctor flicks through his dictionary and points to a phrase. "Conditioned reflex." A tidy, rational theory for an experience that is utterly irrational and deeply disturbing. I already know I won't sleep tonight. So we settle at a food stall instead and talk the night away.

Don't try to explain Indonesia, says Tjiptono. How can anyone understand a country where even the president believes in spirits? Where every banyan holds a *demit?* Where sorcery, black magic, and the supernatural are a way of life?

There are *memedi*, the phantoms who walk at night. They look like headless chickens or skeletons or bald babies. There are *lelembut*, the invisible spirits who enter people and possess their souls. Their evil presence can bring sickness, insanity, even death. There are *tujul*, who mediate between man and the devil. Their subjects grow rich and prosper, suffer agonizing deaths, and must, each year, propitiate the demon with dead bodies.

In this occult half-world, crawling with fear and superstition, medical doctors are usually helpless. Their pills and injections don't work. If they have an answer, then the question is invariably wrong. For this is the uncontested province of the *dukun*, who dutifully propagate and perpetuate the people's anxieties. After all, it's their living.

A top-class *dukun* looks, dresses, and behaves just like his victims. He's simply invested with psychic or more sinister powers. The more credulous say a *dukun* can make people fly, turn them into tigers, and make thieves invisible. Which may be true. For in one hotel, I had my wallet emptied three days in a row.

For a fee, a *dukun* will put spirits in a basket, which then grows heavy and rattles, or bewitch a coconut doll, which, untouched, writes down your fortune. He will cure lumbago with mercury drops and conjure up long-dead ancestors with incense. And for a higher fee, he will cast love spells, fight back a rival *dukun*'s magic, inflict incurable sorrow or illness on an enemy. In a few cases, he will commit murder.

Even Tjiptono, who is skeptical, still has his qualms. Two months ago, a woman collapsed in his surgery with serious abdominal pains. She told him she'd refused to marry a certain *dukun*, who promptly hexed her. In sadistic detail, the enraged witch doctor admitted he had scattered opium and snake's blood in a circle, then dropped broken glass, wire, and sharp tacks at the center. When Tjiptono operated, he found both glass, wire, and sharp tacks.

As it is, even the big, new tourist hotels have had their creepy days. In one isolated hostelry, European visitors kept seeing "white apes" in the corridors, waiters who walked through solid walls and elevator doors. In another, guest suites kept phoning for soap or towels. When the maid reached the room, there was nobody there. The suite was, anyway, unoccupied. Improbable? Maybe. Yet on each occasion, the Western manager summoned a *dukun*, who exorcised the demons and installed a precautionary shrine. And the trouble stopped.

The cities are superstitious, but the countryside, where each moonlit tree and cloud can be mistaken for a monster, is downright obsessed. Whether Muslim, Hindu, or Christian, villagers also idolize every rock and ruin that has "mystery." They place gifts before a charmed bamboo thicket, then pray for health, wealth, or a safe trip. They carry amulets, worship their ancestors' tombs, and at times even make a living sacrifice. On Mount Bromo, a three-day hike from Surabaya, the fearful villagers hold Black Masses on the volcano's rim, then toss live bulls into the molten crater. Just to keep the "fire gods" quiet.

In a country that was doggedly colonized for 350 years, the most eerily mysterious are still the forbidden "black" villages of Badui. The Dutch warily ignored them, and so does Suharto. Only half an hour by helicopter from Djakarta, the tribes of Badui have never entered world society. Isolated in jungly hills, they wear their own black batik, never cut their hair, never touch money, and never leave their territory. They have lived alone since time began. The tribes worship the fountainhead of the river Bantung and think they are its god-appointed guardians. If the source is destroyed, the world will end.

Over the years, explorers have cut through the Badui jungle for days on end, only to find they've been inexplicably misdirected. Several have never returned. A handful found the secret villages, but the people had already vanished. Other explorers, who grew too insistent, died mysteriously. Struck down by a car, poisoned, or insane. A French anthropologist, about to publish a paper, killed himself. Only last year.

"Badui has mystery," says Tjiptono. "Black mystery."

■12■ It's 4 A.M. and the food stall is closing. Tjiptono finds me a room and an army cot. There are cockroaches on the floor, cobwebs on the ceiling. I kick off my shoes and collapse. I'm suffering from mystic overkill.

Surabaya, I'm assured, has wondrous sunrises. Big deal.

■13■ Sleepless and bug-eyed, I stumble out of the bathroom at 5 A.M. and there's a girl in my armchair. "Good morning," she purrs. "I'm Rani." She's got hands tucked under her knees, almond eyes, and a thick, glossy pile of raven hair. She's exceedingly pretty. "I'm coming with you," she adds casually. Now this kind of offer simply doesn't happen in Indonesia. Nice girls don't proposition strange men, and anyway, at 5 A.M. it's downright preposterous.

It had, it turns out, all started when I told Tjiptono that I wanted to take a bus to Bali. No reason. A bus just sounded nice. Even Anglo-Saxons get impulsive in these parts. But the buses, as usual, were full. So Tjiptono had sent me Rani, and she's twenty-two and a law student and has an uncle who has a jeep, and she's got the morning off, and wouldn't I like to see the Baluran Game Reserve instead? So what do you do? And four or five hours later, a battered jeep does miraculously appear, and at one minute's notice, we're off and soon bowling down the coast road.

How far is Baluran? She doesn't know. Where will we stay? She doesn't know. Has she been there often? No, never. Then why are we going? Because it's there. The road is both corrugated and pot-holed, and since our driver is hitting seventy, there's no more time for small talk. In the back, we've got three spare canisters of gasoline, and they're merrily slurping all over. The stench is terrible. But our driver just lights another stogie, tossing the match over his shoulder. He's much too busy playing hit-or-miss with rival kamikaze.

We graze a bus, sideslip a scooter or two, miss a truck by inches. Rani smiles sweetly and takes my hand. We plow through a buffalo herd, sideswipe an army tank, and lose some paint. To keep busy, I'm teaching Rani the words to Weill's "Surabaya Johnnie," and somehow we dodge our sixth truck in a row. Our luck is holding. On which there's an appalling screech and the crack of impact. With convulsive spasms, the jeep shudders to a halt. This time it's a bull's-eye. We've lost both our right fenders, which the driver nonchalantly picks up and throws in the back. "He's used to driving trucks," says Rani.

Five hours later, we're hopelessly lost. Weren't we meant to stop in Bezuki? Or was it Situbondo? Nobody remembers. So what's more logical than to press on *another* fifty miles? Which we promptly do. We swing right then left then right then abruptly turn tail, and after two hours, we're back where we started. We ask a policeman. "You're late for lunch," he says. Inexplicably, there's a flower-strewn table ready for fifteen on the beach and we sit down to a seventeen-course *rijstafel*, the national dish. We're the only guests. I've given up trying to understand. Tjiptono was right: don't try.

During lunch, Rani's jeep drives off and is never seen again. We're stranded. Rani smiles sweetly and shrugs her shoulders. Two hours pass, nothing happens; then another jeep mysteriously draws up. The driver says nothing, but eventually admits he's a third cousin of the fugitive. So we climb in. No, he doesn't know Baluran, but maybe it's *this* way. He improvises various sorties which end in the rice paddies, then sullenly settles for the coast road.

For four hours, we run between columns of coconut palms, close to a dazzling white beach with turquoise surf and scattered pirogues, then climb steeply through teak and mahogany forests, winding between pitch, volcanic boulders, and a bleak, lunar landscape. Darkness falls, Rani sleeps, and our driver is mumbling irritably. Clearly we're in the middle of nowhere and irretrievably lost. Then a flashlight cuts the night. Outside a mud pillbox, Ensign Alidin and Balok the Hunter are waiting. For us. How and why, I will never know. "Salaam," they chorus, and as an extra welcome, Alidin flicks on his pocket tape recorder. Tonight's choice: Dean Martin.

■14■ It's now 4 A.M. and Rani is scared silly. We're perched on a high, creaking watchtower that sits on a hilltop between three live volcanoes. The earth doesn't rumble, but it might, and every time a *tjitjak* lizard croaks, Rani jumps. It's chilly, lonely, and the rustling night echoes with eerie sounds. The jungle chatters, chirps, and squeals, and at times, there's a throaty howl. "Panther too damn noisy," says Alidin, and plugs the tape recorder into his ear.

Still without sleep, we're watching for wild game. But all

we've seen so far is a pack of prairie dogs, buffalo steaks for dinner, and Balok's splendid leopard skin. The moon hides stubbornly behind the clouds, I've got cramps, and anyway, Baluran is hardly the Mount Kenya Safari Club.

From the highway, we'd jogged fifteen miles over a pitted, winding track which dipped and climbed like a roller coaster. Branches scraped the windows, wild chickens scattered and took flight, and just occasionally our wheels bumped over a passing python; the lodge is but a ramshackle, wooden wreck with dirt floors and iron cots, three acetylene lamps, and tarantulas on the ceiling. Baluran is no bunkhouse for the Beautiful People.

Alidin is conditioned to wild boars charging through his backyard and each night beats his bed for lurking cobras. Like game wardens everywhere, he's also both fond and proud of his charges. So before sunrise we down scalding mugs of black Java coffee, Alidin loads his Beretta, and Balok briskly hones his machete. "We don't see tiger often," he says, "but they sometimes nasty." And as day begins, our jeep claws its way across a sweeping, sun-bleached plateau that might be Tanganyika. Rolling savanna, clusters of wispy acacia—and the going is rough. We're driving over knobbly, rock-hard lava that rattles the bones and makes bronco riding feel like a massage.

The sky flushes pink, and as if by signal, the whole landscape suddenly stirs into life. *Banteng* wild oxen, *kerbau* buffaloes, and spindly *muntjak* deer drift placidly across the parched grassland. The mighty herds are moving to their water holes.

By chance, we drive an emerald covey of peacocks from the underbrush. Tiny heads craned, plumage trailing, they dash away like so many flustered ballerinas, leaping gracefully with long, elegant strides. On a slope, a vast procession of deer, maybe a thousand or more, sniffs the air, then pauses. They stand motionless and stare, limpid-eyed and trembling with tension. We draw within fifty feet, walking barefoot and silent. The king stag frisks his tail. His antlers quiver.

Then Alidin shouts: "Look out!" His Beretta cracks. The panicky deer bound away, hooves clicking in mid-air. At Rani's feet, we find a writhing, coiling heap. It's a krait, whose poison can kill in minutes, and Alidin puts a second bullet through its scaly head. "No trouble!" he says cheerfully. "Snake much worse than buffalo."

So we give lunatic chase to a herd of *kerbau*, stampeding them left and right randomly across the plain. Their galloping hooves pound as they wheel and turn, and Alidin is ecstatic. The buffaloes' horns are sharp and slanted, but they seldom fight. So we go bait the wild oxen instead. "They most dangerous in all world," chortles Alidin.

Bouncing like a ping-pong ball, our jeep rides down the eddying herd. Java's *banteng* are enormous. They weigh two tons or more, stand high as a man, and their massive, crescent-curved horns can pierce steel. The oxen move like an army. The hulking, black bulls cover the flanks, and when we come too close, they turn and face us. "Stay in jeep," warns Alidin. The bulls paw the ground but don't move. "If you get out," says Alidin, "they charge. I know." And he shows me a scarred forearm.

With childish glee, Alidin drives the jeep slowly forward. A monstrous bull is only six feet away. His black nostrils flare. He stamps his hooves, snorts, and flicks his tail. Alidin jumps out. The bull tosses his horns and attacks. He misses our friend by an arm's width, turns, and charges again. Alidin sidesteps neatly, tugs the bull's passing tail, then bolts back into the jeep. "You see," he says, all smiles. "Baluran just like Spain!"

■15■ Over the campfire, Balok tells me a fable. An Indonesian fable.

A water buffalo and a scorpion meet on a mud bank. They're stranded by dangerously rising flood waters.

"Hello," says the buffalo. "I'm leaving."

"Can I ride on your back, please?" asks the scorpion.

The buffalo hesitates, then tosses his horns.

"I don't trust scorpions. You'd probably sting me with your tail!"

"Don't be foolish," says the scorpion. "That would be most unreasonable. Then we'd *both* die!"

The old buffalo's eyes narrow, and he gives the matter much thought.

"All right," he says finally.

So the scorpion jumps on the buffalo's back, and they plunge into the raging waters.

Then, halfway to nowhere, the scorpion sinks his poisoned tail into the buffalo's haunch.

End of fable.

■16■ When do Indonesians sleep? It's an interesting question. Maybe they don't. That damn shadow play droned on until Amir the Storyteller lost his voice. Three hours after dawn.

Back at the bunkhouse, Rani is frying peacock eggs for breakfast, and Alidin has locked himself into the toilet nursing his hangover. Balok's leopard skin now crawls with flies—but I'm going to get some shut-eye if it kills me. Balok has other ideas. He wants to take me for a jog trot in the jungle. Good grief! I haven't had even a cat nap for three days, and my legs feel like elastic bands. But he thinks it's more important I should know how to make a pair of sandals from pandanus leaves, and I'm too limp to argue.

So for three hours we stumble over fallen trees, tramp through rotting ferns and fungus, get savaged by mosquitoes; and I dutifully learn how to weave a basket from wild rattan, how to use lianas as rope, how the *dadap* tree can be tapped for a gallon of drinking water. And when we stagger back to the lodge, Rani smiles sweetly and tells me the jeep has gone. Again. "He just got up and went," she says, slightly baffled. Which means we're stuck, once and for all. So we sit down to breakfast, which consists of fried rice, soggy hunks of bamboo, and curried goat.

I see myself a skeleton wasting away on an iron cot, watched by a hundred tarantulas. I glumly wonder how Marco Polo fared when he reached Java. No jeeps in 1292, I keep repeating, so I guess I'll also have to walk. The empty hours drag past and Rani is sulking, when there's an abrupt crunching of tires, and a four-wheeled junk heap clatters into the yard. Its doors are mysteriously marked UNICEF, but nobody asks any questions. We load the suitcases and blast off. Alidin had trekked fifteen miles to the highway and somewhere, somehow, has found a machine that moves.

"We go to Bali," says Balok, fondly patting his machine-pistol. We've wasted five hours, however, and now there's just forty minutes to catch the last ferry boat. It's impossible, but Alidin knows better. He guns the engine, which splutters, groans, and belches smoke; and fully three hours later, we finally see the mist-hung, craggy outline of Bali—The Isle of Light, The Island of a Thousand Temples. Like a cargo of tin cans, we rattle down the wharf, and as happens in Indonesia, the ferry has *not* sailed. We dump the car and sprint up the gangplank. This grimy, rusting hulk, it turns out, had sprung a leak, but Balok prods the skipper and we're away.

A breeze gently ruffles the sapphire straits; its waters glitter and sparkle in the evening sun. Dhows with huffed sails slice across our bow, the gulls are diving, and I watch the looming coastline with dreamy suspense. Bali, Bali, Island of the Gods, Isle of Paradise, Morning of the World. And we land in a desert.

Like Tahiti, I'd rashly expected dancing girls, a kiss on the cheek, at least a welcoming lei. Instead we find a deserted pier, two decrepit buses, a truck or so, arid acres of leveled mud, and no taxis. So we tackle the first bus driver. Will he be driving to Denpasar? Maybe. Maybe not. We tackle the second. Maybe. If the bus gets filled. He's got four clients so far, but it's an eighty-five-mile ride. Then he makes an offer. If we buy forty-five tickets to Denpasar, it's a deal. I tell him his bus only *has* thirty seats. Nuts, says the driver, forty-five tickets or nothing. How about those standing?

"It's the custom," says Rani.

It's growing dark, so we try the truck drivers. Why don't we go to Singaraja instead? says the first. I'm already full, says the second. Three cows, nine goats, and twenty-seven people. All right, says the third, and gouges us fifty cents a head. So we clamber up the truck's tailgate and settle on top of seven tons of sugar cane. But we're not alone. There are eight other adults, three babies in baskets, and formal introductions take place.

In a cloud of dust, our truck pulls out like a Grand Prix dragster. We stumble and slither across the tarpaulin, clutching the only rope, meshed in a sliding heap of arms, legs, loaded weapons, and runaway suitcases. Panic. Pitching and rolling, we careen madly down the straights, drift the corners, bounce, bump, and crash, charging through the night with the wind in our ears. A baby's landed in my lap and I've just poked a grannie in the eye when Balok asks politely, "Do you often do this?"

We edge round sheer cliffsides with oceans pounding, sneak over swaying bridges with inches to spare and a river gorge one hundred feet below. Past tight ranks of coconut palms, past pink, rain-washed temples and snug villages nestling in foliage. The backdrop is beautiful and Gauguin-lush, but lurching fifteen feet above ground at sixty, all you feel is panic.

Then after three hellraking hours, our truck abruptly halts. Our demon driver gets out and vanishes into the jungle. No explanation, nothing. We wait ten minutes, thirty minutes, an hour. Demon driver returns in underpants. He's been having a shower and shampoo under his favorite cascade. An hour later, we stop again. Our lights have blown. Another hour later, and we stop again. Time for drinks. Stiff and aching, we totter to a roadside stall. Our driver smacks his lips and gulps down three glasses of brackish green fluid: coconut water, mushed beans, and condensed milk. "Very delicious," he says. Five other times we get stopped by the police. They don't want drivers' licenses, just cash. So we bribe them seven cents to pass the roadblock, and they look happy.

At 3 A.M. we reach blacked-out Denpasar, where our chauffeur drops us outside a bordello. "We must go see the governor," Alidin says improbably. So we trudge three miles to the governor's mansion. But His Excellency is ailing and the lieutenant-governor is away. Come back at 7:30, says an aide, and offers us the lawn for a bedchamber.

At the police station, I plead for a taxi. The hotel is still eight

Like terraced swimming pools, glassy rice fields mirror the skies above. Mile after mile, the bounteous paddies spread across Java's flooded plains. The rains come, and the young shoots sprout. The sun shines, and the grains ripen. Djakarta may be hungry, but who cares? An indulgent nature keeps the storehouses groaning and bellies full. Rice is the opium of the people. ▶

miles away. "Just a moment," they say, "we make telephone." But the phones are all broken. Anyway, adds the sergeant, there *are* no taxis at night. Thirty minutes later, he's more candid. Actually, he says, there are no cabs during the *day* either. Checkmate. And although I'm attuned to Asia's ways, my sweet temper finally snaps. I charter two pony traps, and we trit-trot off to the beach.

Grimy, disheveled, and caked with dust, toting diverse bags and weapons, we hobble into the marbled lobby of Indonesia's most sumptuous hotel. The deskman, immaculate in blue suit and silver tie, looks us over, then suavely comments: "Ah, yes . . . Mr. Lucas. We were expecting you. Two weeks ago, wasn't it?"

He is, of course, quite right. But how could *he* know that Rani, who came for a morning's drive, hasn't been home for three days, that Ensign Alidin has deserted his post, and that Balok will find a *demit* in his suite?

For my part, I've no problems. It's only my fourth day without sleep.

17

Balok had a restless night. His air-conditioner rattled, and even the manager couldn't convince him it wasn't a demon. Hours before dawn, he was seen prowling the hotel's landscaped gardens, dodging furtively behind the camellias, taking potshots at passing seagulls with his Stechkin. His first night in a bed wasn't a success.

Being a sophisticate, Alidin was more amenable. He took five showers, ate four breakfasts, and tucked a hotel towel under his shirt. He also made his call on the governor, pleaded emergency

◄ *Hemingway would have flipped. On the isle of Madura, off Surabaya, the bulls don't fight—they race. Yoked in pairs, these magnificent bulls cover one hundred meters in nine seconds flat, faster than any living Olympic sprinter. Before the races, the contenders get bathed, brushed, and tenderly massaged. They're fed honey and medicinal herbs, beer by the quart, and raw eggs by the dozen. But there's a price to pay. During the races, the bulls get flogged mercilessly with thorns and nail-spiked rods, and sometimes die from shock. Winners get a stick of cane sugar; losers go to the abattoir. That's life.*

duties, and touched him for a thousand *rupiah*. "It's the custom," said Rani.

And that evening, my loyal escorts hitchhiked back to Java. It had been a super outing, we all agreed, but Rani burst into tears. She thought we were getting married. Ten plus one equals nine.

BALI

1 Bali is bliss.

Bali is *sachertorte* and freshly baked rolls, creamy veal cutlets and *fondue à la bourguignonne*. It's downy beds and hot, flowing water, electric light and pink limousines with capped chauffeurs. After the past week, I feel as out of place as a half-starved bumpkin from Ulan Bator. But contrasts make progress, quoth William Blake, and I'm adapting fast. Wallowing in luxury, eyes closed, spread-eagled by the shimmering pool, I keep banging gongs for waiters who actually materialize, then indulgingly order yet another chilled papaya juice. Nothing can disturb my rapture today.

"Manila, Singapore, Phnom Penh. Seen 'em all. But this Bali, it's so . . . so exotic!"

"*Ja*, but where is the elephants?"

"That's Thailand, *liebchen*."

"*Ah, so desu ka?*"

"*Et les enfants*. So cute, no?"

"*Oui, cherie*. And you drop the Leica in the Ganges. *Merde, alors!*"

"This year we're round the world. Next year we'll go someplace else."

"*Ah, so desu ka?*"

Between the striped parasols, the globe-trotters stretch motionless. French, English, German, and Japanese. Drowsy chitchat dissolving in the heat.

Unlike Java, Bali has been discovered by world tourism, which means twice-a-day dance shows, Bali Night buffets, gift-wrapped batik, and rowdy cruise ships from Sydney. It also means outriggers for hire, mass-produced handicrafts, and hotel checks to match Cannes or Hawaii. Yet it's a peaceful invasion. Despite her languid, flexible nature, Bali can be obstinate and self-possessed. She has the wit to absorb visitors painlessly and to resist change; and like any gorgeous female, she's getting her way.

Besides being charming, gentle, and beautiful, Bali has order. Like a Tuscan hillside, her woods and fields are precise and tidy, as if every vista had been contrived by a landscape gardener. The rippling rice paddies interlock in gracious symmetry, the bamboo has been trimmed, and even the banyans look neat. Mile after mile there's a quality of permanence and timeless harmony, an assurance that any conflicts were settled centuries, maybe millennia, ago. And the countryside reflects the people. Orderly, aesthetic, and secure.

Within the tumult of Indonesia, Bali exists in a vacuum. It's tamer than Java and infinitely more tranquil. Sybaritic maybe, obstinately medieval—yet it's also the ultimate reminder of Indonesia's symbiosis between art, religion, and life. The relaxed, honey-skinned Balinese are a race of "cultured peasants." Each and every farmer is an artist and vice versa.

Victimized by Islam, the asthenic Majapahit dynasty fled Central Java in 1478 and took refuge in Bali. The uncrowned monarch brought his serene Hindu religion and a highly civilized retinue of priests, artists, and courtiers. And ever since, hardly a digit has changed. On an island which is just 2,000 miles square, there are 10,000 temples but no railway, 2,000 dance troupes and no trade union, 60 holidays a year and no compulsory Ramadan. There's not a tractor in sight, yet every village has its own gamelan. Farmers who plant rice by day wash their hands, then make music with virtuoso flair. In a way, its the mood of the kibbutz.

■ **2** ■ I'd vowed to sleep by the pool for three days, but Tilem the Wood Carver soon tempts me away. He keeps tugging my beach towel, eyes laughing. Tilem is not only Bali's most inventive and articulate sculptor; he's also contagiously proud of his island. "I want to show you *my* Bali," he says. "You shall be a guest in my house." So I am.

Drowned in trees and flowers, Mas is the wood-carvers' village. Tilem's family home has neither electricity nor hot showers, yet it has a charm and honesty which no luxury can redeem. Behind high, pink-washed walls draped with bougain-villaea, behind a massive, sculpted doorway, Tilem draws me into an art director's dream world, a pastel mirage of rococo pavilions and miniature, moss-grown courts. Here there is no order, just fancy running wild.

Between flowering shrubs and feathery clumps of bamboo, my bedroom stands like a catafalque, an intricately carved bier for sleeping. Everything seems scattered. Randomly, yet right. Bleached driftwood and toy-sized temples smoking with in-cense, slumbering dogs and cages filled with *perkutut* singing birds. Teak tables sprinkled with frangipani, skittering lizards, and a fragrant, open-air kitchen. Drums, gongs, and fearsome wooden dragons. Branches that sway under a dozen parakeets and an uncounted host of twittering budgerigars. A tropical hothouse designed for living. Witty, theatrical, and enchanting.

From an alfresco fourposter shaded by a fringed canopy, Tilem's father, a skinny, silver-haired gentleman, rises, knots his sarong, and bids me welcome. Like his ancestors, he's a gifted wood carver and the village chief. He's also a Brahmin, the top rung in the Hindu caste system, which the Balinese fondly preserve, and, like his son, entitled to the honorific Ida Bagus instead of plain Mister. Like a medieval autocrat, Tilem Sr. runs the wood-carvers' guild, dispenses justice, settles fam-ily quarrels, and ignores the government. In Mas, his word is law, and even his son, who is thirty-two and married, treats him with deference.

Margaret Mead and Vicky Baum discovered Bali in the early thirties, but nothing has really changed. We're lounging and sipping sour rice wine when the hollow log, which hangs from the village signal tower, booms its call, and everybody begins drifting to the playhouse. A thatched roof, twelve posts, and a floor polished by generations of bare, dancing feet. "It's time for the *legong* rehearsal," says Tilem Jr., who is both village choreographer, costume designer, and stage manager. Next week, it just happens, Mas begins a nine-day festival to propitiate the more dangerous spirits.

The gamelan warms up lazily, then without warning bursts into catatonic action. Sixteen men hammer their xylophones with fierce, staccato rhythm. In wild counterpoint, the gongs force a half beat. A devil's tattoo with tom-toms pounding. In Java the gamelan music is slow, lambent. In Bali it's electrifying. Percussive, syncopated, very fast, and very loud. Crackling waves of deafening sound. "It's Bali's version of the Saber Dance," says Tilem. "Now you'll see my sisters dance." And he claps twice.

Murtini, Sasih, and Wirati. Delicate and delectable. Vibrant as butterflies. Their eyes flicker and slim fingers flutter. Their bare shoulders are deepest amber. Firm young bodies pressed into shimmering, peacock brocades, black hair braided with flowers, gold bracelets tinkling. Weaving and bobbing, they trace feather-light arabesques against the gamelan's throbbing pulse. Flowing yards of trembling gold floating in weightless space. Mysterious, remote, and hauntingly glamorous. Three visions, and Wirati is downright ravishing.

"My god, I'm in love!" I gasp, and I'm only half joking. Tilem smiles. So after the show we move backstage, and I'm struck speechless. Half an hour ago, these dozen girls glowed like golden goddesses. Now they've wiped off their makeup and are earnestly packing their fantastic costumes into bamboo-weave baskets. They're barefoot and dressed in tatty cotton sarongs. Just a bunch of plump, giggly peasant girls who like to dance. Tilem drags me towards a full-breasted girl with dimples and flat feet. "This is my sister Wirati," he says. "She's nine!"

Tilem senses my shock. "Our girls begin dancing when they're five or less," he explains, "and when they marry, they stop.

Since Balinese girls often marry at fourteen, our dancers *must* be young." In Indonesia, I'm learning, it's wiser to curb your intuitions.

3 Next morning, I'm waked at dawn by the chirruping birds. Tilem knocks ever so softly. "Let's go," he whispers. We jump on his motor scooter and frisk into the crisp, crystal morning. The pale sun barely grazes the horizon, yet everywhere there is movement. In the sparkling streams, the villagers bathe and children splash. Small boys with bamboo poles drive the family's ducks to market, others straddle enormous gray water buffaloes. Dusky girls with swaying hips saunter bare-breasted down the roadside, baskets of mangoes balanced on their heads. And as we pass, they modestly cover themselves with a batik shawl.

Squatting on his porch, an old man massages the legs of his fighting cock, his wife sweeps the dirt yard, and their daughters tend a stall heaped with split coconuts. In the rice fields, coolie-hatted peasants toil with simple, hand-made hoes, and in several paddies, whole villages have turned out to harvest a neighbor's crop. Working briskly, they will finish by nightfall and collect ten percent of the market price.

"You see," says Tilem, over his shoulder, "we don't *pursue* anything. We have our own rhythm. We help each other. We allow things just to happen. We don't need money or politicians. God and hard work provide. The rains come, the rice sprouts, and we are happy."

Bounding like a billy goat, our scooter swings into a narrow, idyllic valley where the lush, terraced paddies glisten like myriad swimming pools, where the homes and temples are coral pink, where the tufted palm fronds glisten silver. And in the hazy distance broods the jagged, purple hulk of Gunong Agung, the sacred mountain. Rising 10,000 feet above the sea, the volcano blew its cone six years ago, and a black crust still clings to its rim. It's the stuff of dreams and a view that has already turned a few heads.

Despite its majesty, Gunong Agung is a mean mountain. Its eruption took 1,600 lives, made 87,000 homeless, and blew hot, choking dust all over Bali. Yet the people didn't complain. Known as the Navel of the World, the volcano is also the home of their supreme god, Ida Sang Hyang Widhi Wasa, and his 1,001 manifestations. So the people simply heaped triple mounds of mangoes and rice cakes on their backyard altars, and hoped for the best.

So far, Gunong Agung has kept its temper, but Tilem, who's been to Manhattan, Disneyland, and other distant places, isn't taking any chances. On our way home, we drop off at the holy spring in Bedulu. Tilem knots a batik scarf around my waist, lights a dozen joss sticks, then splashes our faces with spring water. "I'm not really superstitious," he admits grudgingly, "but it's the custom. And anyway, you never know. Do you?"

■ 4 ■ Back at Tilem's house, the wood carvers are already at work. They squat on bamboo mats, three dozen or more, nonchalantly chiseling. Clever fingers chip away until the ebony block takes shape. Others sand and polish. We breakfast quickly off black coffee, sticky rice, and guava jelly, then Ida Bagus Tilem moves among his workers. Perched on his heels, he quietly advises on the angle of an arm, the contour of a dancer's face. "Softer, softer," he keeps saying. In the lumber yard Tilem picks a log, examines it carefully, and chalks an impulsive outline. "This will be a woman," he says. "Kneeling. Hands crossed. Like so." Then with sharp, precise blows, he chops the wood with a small ax. The craftsmen nod with approval.

Besides guiding his team of wood carvers, Tilem also makes his own abstract sculptures, which can be pricey. Yet he gives away as much as he sells. "Now maybe you understand Bali," he

Happiness is sloshing in the mud and sluicing down your father's buffalo. ▶
In a muddy, sun-drenched river, two young boys make sure that the hard-worked beast enjoys a restful afternoon. In the countryside, schools are still dispensable luxuries. So are pants.

says. "Muslims are warriors. They like to fight. We Hindus prefer peace. We revere it. We think a single lotus is more important than a hundred mushroom clouds."

5 Bali is the kind of place you want to keep secret. After
a few days, tiny doubts begin curling through your
mind. And you start to wonder. Yes, why not? Why
not turn to jelly? Why not stake out a base camp under the
coconuts? Why not pass the daylight hours combing the
beach for seashells? And the starry nights entwined in the musky
limbs of some Balinese nymphet? Yes, dammit, why not? The
island is enchanting, you keep telling yourself, the climate balmy,
and the natives friendly. So why not? What is so important in
the big outside? The taxes? The carbon monoxide? The shows
you'll never see?

I caught the virus from Hans Snel, who's a painter. He came
for a weekend and never left. That was twenty-two years ago.
Snel was shipped to the East Indies to fight Sukarno's guerillas.
He was a Dutch army officer, but he threw in the towel instead.
In Ubud, the village of painters, Snel now has an exquisite Balinese wife, a lotus pond, an art gallery, and an Indonesian pass-
port. "I'm a white-skinned Indonesian," he says, "and I've no
regrets." Snel works in oils and five years ago junked his cam-
eras, hi-fi, tape recorders, and electric generator. "Technical
things are a bloody bore," he explains. "Machines simply com-
plicate living."

Slouched in a canvas chair, Snel fairly exudes contentment.
He's in his mid-forties, deeply tanned, handsome; and he looks
intolerably fit. He's wrapped in a sarong, wears no shoes. He has
five servants, two motor scooters, and a pair of adorable, saucer-
eyed children. He's taught his ravishing wife to use mascara and

◀ *Young faces. Happy faces. Innocent yet assured, they still haven't learned
about cumshaw and corruption. They still don't know that their life span is
tragically short. Maybe thirty-two or less. Yet there's consolation. Like all
Oriental children, they're shamelessly spoiled and pampered. They're also
wickedly adorable.*

darken her fluttery lashes. Otherwise she's uneducated. Her name is Ni Made Siti, and she's scrumptious as a honeyed cream puff.

"What's her age?" says Snel. "God only knows. Probably around twenty-six. Actually, I kidnapped her. I saw her working in the paddy and she looked good. So a few days later, I took her by force. It's the custom. She screamed and kicked a bit, but I got her to the priest anyway. Her parents made an awful howl. It's expected, you know. Then after a week's haggling, they graciously consented." Snel fondly thwacked her luscious rump. "We're pretty happy, aren't we, baby?" Ni Made Siti twitched her toes, flickered those enormous lashes, and wriggled deeper into her sarong.

Snel isn't exactly slumming. He owns about five acres; a rambling, tiled home with cool, spacious rooms; a vine-clung patio; a rolling stretch of emerald lawn hedged with banana trees; and the only sunken bathtub in Bali. Snel hasn't been to Djakarta in a decade, sensibly shuns politics in favor of beach picnics. As a painter, he doesn't strain himself. "I have to push myself," he admits. "Inspiration through transpiration. That's the way of the tropics." Snel works when he pleases, dabbles in wispy landscapes, yet sells enough to pay the bills. In an imperfect world, he's got it made.

Enthralled, appalled, my eyes grow misty, and I see Snel, enthroned like a Persian satrap, waited on by nubile, obsequious maidens, nibbling peeled grapes, toping nectar from golden goblets, airily flicking paint at a hundred canvases. Then my temper snaps. Yes, dammit. Me too. To hell with it all. Why should *I* work? Why should *I* worry? Why should *I* mess around with a civilization that's forever chewing its own tail? Yes, dammit. Me too.

■6■ After a rumpled, topsy-turvy night, I wake abruptly, gulp down three cups of coffee, then drive into the dawn. The sunlight filters wanly through the bamboo forests, tidy platoons of ducks still waddle down the roadside, and opalescent mists hang motionless over the glassy paddies.

It's dreamy as all get-out. Airline poster stuff. And Snel is right, I keep repeating. He's no eccentric, just a realist. But I'll take a second opinion anyway. Paco Maria Santos, known as Narciso. Another painter. Another blissful fugitive. Or so I'm told.

We cross a stream and climb a sharp hill, dodge nimbly between a grunting confusion of pigs and two rickety gift stalls. The sows are battleship gray and their bloated bellies swing obscenely, like monstrous udders. A toothless crone shoves a bolt of batik under my arm, but I break away. "Mr. Narciso is a famous artist," cautions my guide, Astama. "He's different from other people."

Shangri-la perches on a hilltop, which is only proper for a pleasure dome. The view is devastating. Airy pavilions nestle between the sandalwood trees, the patio floors are tiled with ceramic, and the master personally greets us. Being an artist, Paco Maria Santos, known as Narciso, wears a navy-blue beret, cerise silk shirt open to the navel, silver chain and pendant, and an ankle length, saffron sarong. He pumps my arm till it aches. "Sukarno says Narciso is the world's greatest painter," he announces, "and Sukarno is usually right." Narciso looks like a shrunken Walter Matthau but sounds like Barrymore doing *Man of la Mancha*. Only the windmills are missing.

It is 7 A.M. The master settles cross-legged on a Bokhara rug, claps his hands, and a toothsome maid brings a jug of rice wine. Narciso pours brimming tumblers. "When Narciso has inspiration, he feels like a giant," the master intones, arms flailing. "He can do anything. Anything. His art pours forth like a cataract! Narciso paints what pleases him, and what pleases Narciso pleases the world!" To be precise, Narciso paints flesh—female flesh. Warm, cuddly heaps of amber torsos. Bulging Balinese thighs, arched Balinese hips, and voluptuously thrusting Balinese mammalia. Slightly wicked ("Hey, Marty, dig the freaky tits on this Bali babe!") yet eminently marketable.

Being versatile, Narciso also runs his own Eros Art Gallery, which exclusively presents the master's mixed meats. He fondly treasures his remarkable library of "erotology," which includes Sacher-Masoch in Spanish, and this year for Christmas, he's mailing out phallic woodblocks of the Balinese god Mahlen, who's involved in fertility. The print shows the deity amiably clutching his massive, if hoary, instrument. According to legend, Mahlen goes to war unarmed. When angered, however, he swings his prodigious totem like a knobkerrie and swiftly decimates his foes. "It's *fantástico*, don't you think?" roars Narciso and pours himself another jigger.

Being a very famous artist, Narciso sleeps alone. Each night he hits the sack with Louis-XIV-style protocol: he gets undressed by his maidservants, then solemnly retires into a brocaded, many-tasseled palanquin. He keeps his wife, three daughters, and the other women in a separate compound. The master's eyes twitch naughtily. "The people say Narciso claps his hands in the middle of the night and calls his harem," he guffaws. "And maybe the people are right. Ha, ha, ha!"

The master quaffs his rice wine, then wobbling slightly, rises from his prayer rug. "You shall now meet Narciso's public," he says. Slowly, stiffly, like a match-stick matador, Narciso urges me pridefully round his framed photos of celebrated visitors. A motley collection indeed. H. H. Humphrey from Minnesota, baring his teeth; H. Selassie from Abyssinia, wrapped in a lion skin; John Steinbeck; and Bergman—Ingrid, not Ingmar. "*Hombre!* they are all my friends," whispers the master. And for a moment, he seems almost overcome by his own renown. But the show's losing pace. So Narciso, who knows his melodrama, belts a gong. Loudly, furiously, like a carnival hustler.

Backstage right, enter a woman. She's a frail Balinese with copper skin and almond eyes. Her limbs ripple freely under a loose sarong, and Narciso's eyes rove hungrily over his wife's contours. "Her name is Ni Serodja, which means 'slender lily,' " says Narciso, and he slips a furry hand around her waist. "I first saw her down there. She was planting rice, and I wanted her. It was kismet. I am now building Ni Serodja a temple. It will be splendiferous. It will be better than the Taj Mahal, *caramba!* Shah Jehan built his favorite wife a temple. But she was dead. My Ni Serodja will still be living!"

Narciso's pupils glitter feverishly. But Ni Serodja isn't impressed. She wriggles out of the master's grip. Ni Serodja was up all night baking cookies. Thirty dozen, no less. For the tourists from the Sydney cruise ship. But the buses couldn't make the hill, so the visitors went home. *"Putas!"* howls Narciso. "Those fat, useless old trollops! They couldn't even get up my hill!" The master wrenches off his beret, flings it across the patio, and stalks growling into his chaotically disarranged studio. Exit Narciso.

It's 8:45 A.M. Sunday, and I'm loaded to the gills. So I pour myself another snort. Why not? It's hot, humid; and sweaty beads are trickling into my eyes. Astama has vanished. So has everybody else. I'm alone in paradise. And waiting for the final act.

I'd been warned, and it comes on cue. I hear bare feet padding across the tiles. I turn. It's Ni Serodja's younger sister. She's Narciso's favorite model, and she's been told to show me round the Eros Gallery. Alone.

Shalimar is very beautiful. She is slim, supple, and delectably brown. Thick, lustrous hair tumbles down her bare, golden shoulders. She has high cheekbones, dimpled knees; she walks like a caress. Her sarong doesn't conceal; it suggests. She's a provocative bundle, and she knows it.

Side by side, we drift into the dark, oval chamber. It's shadowy, silent, and the girl does not speak. The heady scent of frangipani hovers around Shalimar. Her deep, liquescent eyes flutter moodily over Narciso's tangled bodies, over the tussling piles of tortured flesh. Her warm, candied lips pucker, then pout sulkily as she examines her own portrait—naked as Eve. Shalimar's lashes flicker, and she half catches my glance. Her arm, smooth as wax, brushes against mine. If the customer looks a winner, Shalimar can be more friendly. Or so I'm told.

I didn't see Narciso again. I only heard his voice. "Tell Picasso to write!" he shouted. "Tell him I'm waiting!" The master's voice bounced eerily through the empty pavilions, and I began to wonder. Was this what Bali did to people? Was McLuhan right, after all—"Art is anything you can get away with"? Good grief! And suddenly Bali's subversive charms began to dissolve. Somehow the place smelt rotten. And I got mad. Mostly with myself.

Paco Maria Santos, known as Narciso, has been prowling this

fool's paradise for seventeen years, and for an artist, he's grooving on the wrong track. He's hung up all right, I keep telling myself, and I angrily crunch the limousine into high. "Mr. Narciso is a very great painter," says Astama. "We're very proud of him." And he smiles graciously, smugly.

At times, these people are intolerable. They're so credulous it hurts. They'll kowtow to the first two-bit dilettante who smudges a canvas. Anything to spin out their own dubious myth.

7 In the tourist syllabary, Bali and Tahiti come wrapped in the same cliché. Paradise. They're both islands, both remote, both unspoiled and filled with sunny, handsome, fun-loving natives. But there the cliché ends. Whatever Gauguin did, whatever the flacks say, Tahiti is, and always has been, a cultural wasteland. With its hippy wahines, demented dancing, and a handful of scruffy tikis, France's Pearl of the Pacific is about as civilized as a Saturday night booze-up at Quinn's Bar, which isn't saying much.

By contrast, Bali is downright refined. Its 2,300,000 people are aristocrats—well bred, courteous, even wise. They share a natural charm and elegance. Unlike Tahiti, they are the proud heirs of an ancient and genuine culture. The credentials are valid, yet the myth is sheer hyperbole. The myth would have Bali typecast as a unique haven where genius sprouts like ragweed. And it just isn't so.

Isolated by time and distance, the Balinese lovingly perpetuate their unending festivals, and at the same time, pacify their distinctly hostile gods. With painstaking, strictly partisan devotion, they faithfully heap their tamarinds into unchanging, symmetric pyramids, plait gold thread into unchanging brocades, weave pandanus into the unchanging fans and baskets that ritual demands. Year after year, they chant the same chants, play the same music, and dance the same dances. The iridescent costumes haven't changed in five centuries. The whole business is as functional as Easter Mass in St. Peter's. It's all very pretty, but it isn't Art.

Maybe it's no coincidence that the island is shaped like a pre-historic turtle. Its life evolves with equal speed. Which means it doesn't. Bali is a living museum piece. This isn't a sin, I know, but it doesn't produce Art. It's skilled handicraft, the work of clever, sensitive fingers—what the Japanese call *kiyo*. The people are artistic, but they're not creative. They're making copies of copies of copies. And thereby perishes a myth. It's probably treason to say so, but the Balinese are mostly making junk. It might look titillating in a Third Avenue curio store, but that's about it.

In Mas, the wood carvers' village, the roadside shelves fairly groan with repetition. Satinwood dancers. By the dozen. Bali-nese deities, couchant or otherwise. By the score. Swan necks, fluted arms, limbs elongated like Modigliani. All neatly tagged and priced. The Gautama's slender hand, sculpted in ebony. Just right for a paperweight. My friend Tilem does superb work, but he hasn't produced in months. He's too busy driving his team of one hundred "cultured peasants," as they deftly chisel lotus-flower ashtrays that will land on a coffee table in Wink, Texas.

In Ubud, the painters' village, the situation is hardly less dreary. Back in the thirties, a few restless, long-forgotten paint-ers, mostly Dutch, settled there and haphazardly introduced the wonders of Western art. They brought small talents, academic tedium, pots of fashionable tempera; and within months, every working male in Ubud was a painter. With sedulous craftsman-ship, they aped the visitors' tricks, then put down what they saw on canvas. The results were flat, washy, vaguely erotic, and they sold. Balinese beauties with naked breasts, their exotic loins modestly draped, luxuriating among tropical shrubs and flowers. And Ubud's pseudo-masters have been plagiarizing themselves ever since. About twenty dollars a square yard.

"They're all on the same track," says Jim Pandy. "The scene is dying out. We've probably got another ten years." Pandy should know. He's the Baron Duveen of Bali, a plump, shrewd promoter who's made three fortunes hustling local folk craft. He's merrily shipping "Made in Bali" to five continents, but he keeps the rare masterworks for himself. "Taste is made by the tourist," says Pandy, implying that Gautama paperweights will soon be dropping from plastic molds. Pandy isn't only knowledgeable. He's also a cynic.

Others are more honestly concerned. Irritated by Ubud's pretensions, Arie Smit, a Dutch painter who's spent more than a decade in Bali, made a valiant effort to shake the place out of its torpor. He recruited a dozen young boys, aged ten or less, gave them canvas and brushes, and told them to paint. "I simply set them loose," Smit remembers, "and they went wild. They had no inhibitions. They used the most violent shapes, colors, textures, and it was very exciting." Ironically enough, the boys produced almost identical stacks of breathtakingly fresh, vivid, primitive paintings—Bali versions of Douanier Rousseau—and they became the rage overnight.

But that was eight years ago, and the boys are now men, and they are still painting the same crude, puerile stuff. End of experiment. "These days, art is seen as saleable," Smit says morosely. "These people aren't lazy, just unthinking. For them, painting is just another job. It's the woman's duty to carry rocks and plant rice. It's the man's duty to train fighting cocks and paint pictures. Amen."

With its airport gone international, with its back roads gone public, Bali is now open to the world's instant shoppers. Another quaint superbazaar for the jumbo-jetting hordes. Suddenly it's a sellers' market, and Bali's tiny world, however trivial, however humdrum, is doomed. The new breed of globetrotters want more than color slides. They want Things for the rumpus room. "Sure, it's plastic, honey. But who'd ever know?"

For Narciso and the others, it's a windfall. They can put up their prices. Becalmed in their lotus land, they don't get much done anyway. The harsh labors of invention don't mesh too easily with idyllic living. It's all too comfortable, too soporific, to think, to work, to create. Too hot, too sultry, too permissive, too damned sexy. Inspiration through transpiration. Yes, it's a nice phrase. But the tropics don't inspire. They destroy.

But the living *is* easy, isn't it? Those plump, juicy guava cost only a few *rupiah*. The surf is sparkling. Indolence isn't a crime.

And there's always tomorrow. And anyway, that sweet Shalimar, that moist, quivering Shalimar will be back after dark. . . .

The Bali Beach Hotel. 11:45 P.M. The bar. Two gentlemen from Beverly Hills. Young swingers. Sideburns. Mod getup. Vodka martinis. Young swingers. Making the scene.

"Sure, Abe. But do they screw?"

"All broads screw."

"Yeah. But here?"

"Aw, c'mon. Didn't you see that waitress give me the eye?"

"So what?"

"So I got a date with her. Day after tomorrow."

"You're putting me on!"

"No, I'm not. But . . ."

"But what?"

"I'm leaving tomorrow. Thai Airlines. 12:30."

Pause.

"Abe, do you think you can take 'em up to the room?"

"Why the hell not?"

"Well, you know . . ."

Pause.

"I bet these Bali chicks really blow your mind."

"Yeah."

"They tell me they're kinda different."

"Yeah?"

"Yeah."

"Where are they different?"

"Aw, c'mon, Abe. You know . . ."

Pause.

"Jeez. But I'd sure like to try."

"Yeah."

"Hell, maybe I could pinch-hit with your waitress?"

"Yeah. Why not?"

"Guess I better ask her first . . ."

"Yeah."

"Which one was it? They all kinda look alike."
Pause.
"I guess she's gone. Must be off duty."
"Yeah."
Pause.
"Well, might as well have one for the sack."
"Yeah."
"Hey, barman, give us two more. And make 'em extra dry, will you?"
Pause.
"Jeez. But I'd sure like to try. Just once."

9 It's one of the minor tragedies of the jet age that a growing posse of young, healthy, moneyed bachelors spend their hard-earned savings on three-week, packaged, round-the-world tours in desperate, salivating pursuit of exotic, untried, and supposedly paradisiacal mating experiences. Reliable polls show that these once healthy, moneyed Romeos return home edgy, haggard, and penniless, big on anecdotes and painfully short on accomplishment. Isn't it a shame? They should learn the rules. In Bali, for instance, every winsome miss past the age of puberty sleeps around with hell-raking abandon, easing her pangs indiscriminately and with absolutely guiltless pleasure. But only with her own kind. The visiting paleface needs at least a third-party introduction. "White gorillas"—that's us. And we smell of mutton, too.

10 You can't really blame them. At the turn of the century, a Dutch gunboat raked Denpasar with cannon, and the people have not forgotten. The jolly burghers landed marines, threw a rifled cordon around the palace, and called for surrender. With dreadful bravado, the Balinese responded in their own way. The palace gates were flung open. Unarmed, barefoot, under a gilded parasol, the reigning prince shuffled his splendidly robed wives, children, and courtiers into the blazing sunshine. The Dutch marines opened fire point-blank, and the cortege was mown down in a hail of bullets. It was a crazy, pointless act of self-immolation. Irrational, fatalistic, Oriental. It was also the nastiest kind of colonial repression, but the Dutch seemed well satisfied. The seven-hundred-year-old Majapahit dynasty had been liquidated in just one minute. So the brick-faced burghers wiped their muskets and sailed home to Surabaya. They were far too busy milking the riches of Java. "We had nothing to offer," Astama observed. "Only rice, coconuts, and the ways of peace."

After this gratuitous correction, the Dutch left Bali alone. So did Sukarno. And so have the Generals.

For his part, the flamboyant, amoral Sukarno used the island mostly as a love nest. Bali's sexuality apparently excited his fantasies. Behind barbed-wire coils, Sukarno built himself a splashy, secretive, Hollywoodsy retreat at Bedulu—twin mansions on twin hills, spanned by a soaring viaduct. The bedrooms had mirrors on the ceiling. Here Sukarno dallied with his newest wives, concubines, and other playmates. Here he spent yummy weekends with his fifth and final wife, Ratna Dewi (née Naoko Nemoto), the piquant Japanese bar girl he picked up in a Tokyo cabaret. "Sukarno loved beauty in all its forms," Astama said reverently.

Being spoilsports, the Generals have put Sukarno's playpen under lock and key, yet they treat Bali with exceptional tolerance. Being pragmatists, they've learned that gum-chewing paratroopers don't exactly inspire a carefree, holiday mood. So their pistol-packing tough guys are kept discreetly hidden. The "white gorillas" must be allowed to splurge their dollars in peace.

Thus Bali goes on its balmy way. In the freak-out which is Indonesia, the festival-a-day isle tenderly cultivates its myths and gardens, leisurely practices its cherished rites, time-consuming habits and diversions. The rat race is for others.

Each morning the Balinese devotedly dress up their household gods. They tactfully cover genitalia with knotted sarongs, maybe place a hibiscus behind a deity's ear. They fill up the god's rice bowl, replenish his wine jug, and generally dust him down. If there's a festival, they'll strap a wrist watch round his arm, even hang a transistor radio round his neck. Anything to make him happy. Ida Sang Hyang Widhi Wasa and his 1,001 manifestations get royal treatment.

In the afternoons, while father grooms his fighting cock, the children fly kites, take the ducks for a walk, scatter across the hills giving chase to dragonflies. The ducks are well regimented. They waddle in single file like marching veterans. Once settled in a paddy, they never stray more than a dozen yards from their parade ground. The children trap the dragonflies with sticky twigs. If it rains, the kids cover their heads with banana leaves. It's a tidy life, and "Order is Heaven's first law."

In the evenings, while the children practice music or dancing, father sloshes through the rice fields with an oil lamp. With wooden pincers, he abruptly strikes into the muddied waters, snapping up a wriggling, eel-like worm. At dinner, the worms get tossed into the family pot. So do frogs, snakes, centipedes, diverse grubs, and the dragonflies. "Protein," says Astama.

Since there are no seasons, one month folds peacefully into the next. The monsoons are punctual, the climate is constant, and the gods stay mostly quiet. The green rice shoots sprout and ripen, the pigs wax fat, and nothing disturbs the tranquil, unchanging routine of centuries. Except the *leyak.*

Bold, dazzling, theatrical Bali. After nightfall, by flickering torchlight, ▶
150 dancers crouch before a pink-swabbed temple. In a shower of gold leaf,
King Rama leaps between his bowed, chanting subjects. No gongs, no
drums; just the staccato, rhythmic chatter of 150 voices. It's Bali's fabulous
ketjak, *the Monkey Dance. Wild, barbaric, awesomely exciting; art and*
religion inextricably intertwined. As happenings go, this is it.

OVERLEAF: *Markets can be a bore, but Bali's are enthralling. In village*
after village, I stumble into riots of color; teeming, busy crowds; and eye-
popping heaps of exotic goodies. Hot chilis and pungent cloves, root ginger
and powdered cinnamon, sandalwood, plover eggs, and curly bean sprouts.
In Denpasar's market, a pregnant lady, bulbously swaddled in a red ban-
dana, suspiciously eyes her stooping neighbor. First: because she's paying
cash. The Balinese prefer to barter. Second: because she's buying a packet of
betel. These scarlet seeds are gently narcotic. When chewed, they stain the
teeth but offer a comforting buzz. Or so I'm told.

At nightfall, the couth, cultured Balinese are all at once seized by paroxysms of terror, haunted by a gibbering infinity of ghosts, goblins, flibbertigibbets, and things that go bump in the night. Despite their sophistication, the Balinese are suckers for the supernatural, and the ubiquitous *leyak* get blamed for everything from laryngitis to busted fenders. "While passing the cemetery at Tandjungbungkaka, the witch Ranga jumped on the hood of the bus," reported one driver. "Disguised as a black cat, her fearful claws caught my throat through the window. My heart stopped, and I ran into the ditch."

The driver has my sympathy. I've seen a mask of Ranga, queen of the witches. She has gnarled fangs, sagging bosoms, and a red leather tongue, eyes like licorice balls, and a wildly matted mane of rancid yellow hair. She would scare the pants off Sir Galahad in broad daylight, and she doesn't funk out lightly. You can either spit, spray her with perfume, or best of all, urinate in her face. In moments of extremity, Ranga is a hard witch to handle.

One dark night, as we drove through the spooky, chattering forest, Astama acted jumpy. He kept wiping his brow, fidgeting in his seat. Two weeks before, he finally confessed, the car ran out of gas here, and he hiked eighteen miles back to the hotel. On the way, in a graveyard in the moonlight, he saw a beautiful, naked girl. Alone. Lounging provocatively against a tombstone. Rashly, Astama tiptoed closer. He came within feet, held out his hand, and his fingers passed clean through her breasts. Then, without a sound, the girl dissolved in a phosphorescent glow. Astama fainted.

"You'll probably never see a *leyak*," Astama smirked. "They're shy with strangers. Like our bullocks, they don't like the white man's smell. But if you're really interested, try standing unclothed in a cemetery at night, then peer backwards be-

◄ *Caught by a morning shower, two barefoot farmers trudge down a deserted highway. The Balinese like to keep their feet cool and their ears dry. So what more natural than to chop down a brace of banana leaves? They're not only cheaper than umbrellas. They're also readily available and instantly disposable.*

tween your legs. That's the best way." I told Astama I wasn't
that anxious.

■11■ The bugaboos probably explain why the people don't
sleep much at night. In the villages, they play cards,
gamble, or sit around glowing embers telling stories.
They prefer an afternoon siesta, when the sun is high and hot
and the midnight phantoms are hiding. Despite the hobgoblins,
life flows smoothly on. All in all, it's a placid, pastoral existence.
Yet it has its upbeat, offbeat moments. Like tooth-filings and
cremations. Filing teeth? Yes. Burning bodies? Yes. They are
Bali's predilected pastimes.

Rather than cosmetic dentistry, tooth-filing is a religious rite.
"No Balinese can be cremated until his teeth have been filed," I
was assured. "Otherwise the gods might mistake him for a
fanged demon and keep him out of Heaven." Being both practical
and richly superstitious, Bali's Hindus have therefore devised a
suitably reassuring ceremonial. When a child reaches puberty,
he is promptly tucked away behind bamboo screens, starved for
a day and a night, then dressed in his finest batik sarong. Next
morning, the priest turns up bearing a mean-looking file and
other orthodontic equipment.

If you've seen one tooth-filing, you've seen them all; and I saw
mine in the village of Redjang. It was more like a kinky form of
exorcism than a visit to the jawsmith, but it was voted a success
anyway. Ni Aty looked scared. She must have been eleven or
less. Wrapped in gorgeous silver and gold sashes, she had been
washed, scrubbed, douched, drained, and wholly purified. Her
eyes were shadowed, brows penciled, lips painted, hair lacquered
with beeswax. And her mouth trembled.

In the courtyard, the gamelan struck up a glum, ghoulish beat.
Ni Aty was thrown down on a low couch. Family and neighbors
crowded round, incense was burned. Ni Aty's sisters firmly
grasped her slim wrists and ankles. The priest rubbed a gold
ring against the girl's lips, mumbling a magic incantation. Then
quickly, roughly, he began grating his tapered file against Ni

Aty's six upper front teeth. Metal screeching against enamel, like thumbtacks against a blackboard. Sheer agony.

The girl winced. Eyelids flickered. But the file kept scraping. White tooth dust flecked the priest's fingers. At times, Ni Aty spat into a coconut shell. The screeching went on for an infinity. Goose pimples freckled down her smooth arms. But the canines were finally even and pretty. Ni Aty clenched her teeth, glanced into a hand mirror, then smiled shyly. "It didn't really hurt," she said, and shivered. The filings were swept up, placed in a casket, and buried behind their home. "Even the teeth hold a part of the soul," they said. Then a blissful grin spread across Ni Aty's face. Her place in Heaven was now assured.

Unless you're a sadist, tooth-filing parties aren't much fun. But cremations are. They're frolicsome as Mardi Gras—riproaring affairs aimed at giving the corpse a festive, rollicking send-off. No tears, no sadness, no mawkish mourning. Just good, clean fun. For the Balinese aren't frightened of death. They sensibly believe in reincarnation. After a well-earned rest in the afterworld, we'll soon be back. "The body is only the basket of the soul." So cremations swing. They're spectacular, carnavalesque countdowns where the human soul gets launched into the hereafter; and many inquiring tourists hang around for weeks just to catch the show.

To date, you can't buy tickets to cremations. You just walk in, which is what I did in Bangli. I was lucky. Cremation parties don't happen every day. They're extravagant fiestas, and they cost a lot of money. Many families keep their corpses buried for years, hopefully waiting for a shindig sponsored by some wealthy, high-caste neighbor. And today's conflagration is no exception. The featured corpse belongs to a rich landowner, and there are eleven attendant cadavers.

Outside the Brahmin's home, the whole village swirls in cheerful confusion. I'm not on the guest list, but nobody minds. An old lady sticks a gardenia behind my ear, smilingly chucks me under the chin. Balanced on their heads, the young girls carry baskets heaped with fruits. There's much banging of gongs, the twang of nose flutes, and friendly jostling. Then sudden silence.

Hands stretched high, a dozen men jogtrot into the street bearing a bundle wrapped in yellow cloth. The crowd shrieks with pleasure. It's the corpse.

Without warning, the villagers of Bangli go berserk. Elbowing, shoving, shrilly howling, they grab the cadaver, whirling it wildly above their heads. The melee turns into a stampede. I get knocked to the ground and trampled. I struggle up. The corpse is now being tossed about like a rag doll. It spins in mid-air, buckjumps, spirals limply into a slow-motion somersault, and a gray arm slips from the bundle. The limb gets tucked back, and the corpse keeps flying. "It's the custom," Astama shouts breathlessly. "The body must be confused. So he can't find his way back into the house. Otherwise he'll haunt his family."

Properly disoriented, the cadaver is next hoisted on top of a forty-foot tower—a gaudy, tinseled scaffold with gilded streamers and paper flowers. Under a clutch of tasseled umbrellas, the once-stately Brahmin is lashed down with ropes; fifty sturdy villagers hoist the whole contraption onto their shoulders, then stumble towards the cemetery. Every fifty yards or so, the lurching, wobbling tower is spun abruptly around. Grandad mustn't find his way home. Never again.

At the graveyard, the village women huddle under a long, white shroud. The fabric ripples like an outsized caterpillar. The corpse is eased down onto the cloth and carried to the funeral pyre, where it is settled, most tenderly, into a sarcophagus shaped like a roaring bull.

For the scheduled trip into the hereafter, the priest provides clothes, food, medicine, and ransom money for Yama, lord of the underworld. Precious brocades, colored rice, and the head of a freshly killed buffalo are arranged about the cadaver. To sharpen the senses, the priest places shivers of mirrored glass on the eyelids (to give them brightness), chips of steel on the teeth (to give them strength), jasmine blossoms in the nostrils (to sweeten the breath), iron nails on arms and legs (to fortify the bones).

The crowd has grown still. In the heat of midday, the colors shimmer and it's hard to breathe. Eleven more coffins are filled with eleven more corpses. They are sprinkled with holy water, then tidily stacked about the kindling wood. There's the smell of death around, and I'm feeling queasy. But it's almost over.

The people chant a final prayer, and the priest lowers a blazing torch into the pyre. The crowd gasps. Dry tinder smolders, then bursts into flame. Orange tentacles coil hungrily up the bull's cardboard sides. The blaze spits and crackles, spewing red-hot cinders. Do I really smell burning meat? I don't know. The fires rage and dance. Sheets of flame scorch our faces. A corpse sits up in its coffin, then explodes in a shower of sparks. The pyre collapses. Black, oily smoke curls high into the sky and the stench is appalling. But nobody cares. They're jigging and laughing and singing and crying with joy. Twelve more Balinese souls are safely on their way. And the night will be spent in feasting.

By our values, it's a ghoulish, macabre, slightly horrible send-off. But the Balinese feel differently. They consider a dazzling, fun-packed cremation their most sacred duty. They are, after all, optimists. Even today, they see Nirvana as a Bali without troubles or sickness and cannot imagine any happier reincarnation than to be returned someday to their own beloved isle. It's both a charming and a touching conceit. In a roughshod world, we can only envy their waking dreams. Naive maybe, but far from foolish.

12

"Hey, Abe, d'ya know that dancing cheek to cheek is banned in Bali?"

"Yeah? Why so?"

"They're too darned sexy."

"Waddayamean?"

"The natives just freak out if they get that close. They get so uptight they gotta screw right away. Any time, anyplace."

"Jeez. Just like me."

We've piled into our pink microbuses, and we're making tracks down the back roads to the village of Peliatan. We're off to see Bali's most publicized happening, the *ketjak*, better known as the Monkey Dance, and the gang's all here. A jolly crew, I must say.

There's Abe and Mort, a robed Nigerian diplomat, a retired French admiral, two slinky Indian air hostesses, and sixty-seven beer-sloshed Aussies. There's a glum honeymoon couple from Japan, a Swiss atomic physicist, an Egyptian date salesman, a granitic widow from Pasadena, and a balding English faggot who decorates bathrooms. It's going to be a great evening, and everyone's agog.

"Have you been sick yet?" asks the widow from Pasadena. I tell her I'm fine.

"That's nice," she says. "Me too. Been gone three weeks and not even a rumble. Just stick to ham and eggs, mister. You can't go wrong."

The bus lurches round an oxcart, scatters a swarm of chickens, then dives down a hillside. We're hitting sixty and making like bronco busters.

"St. Tropez? Yes, luv, isn't it ghastly?" says Mr. Kenneth. "Why, I wouldn't be seen dead in that cesspool!" He smooths down his frilled shirt, bracelets tinkling. "Now Bali . . . that's another cup of tea. Just dreamy, isn't it? And aren't the boys ducky?"

"*Ah, so desu ka?*"

"Yes, dear. Such pretty eyes."

The road flattens out, darkness falls, and a ruddy sunset dapples the clouds. A full moon plays across the rice paddies, brick walls glow like coral, and the French mariner clears his throat.

"Ah, Bali, *île enchanteresse! Quelle métamorphose!* When I bring my cruiser here in '37, the people bear me from the reef on their shoulders. They cover me with flowers, make wonderful music, and feed me baby pigs. And the girls! Ah, the girls. So beautiful and so . . ."

"So what?" snaps Abe.

"So charming, so seductive, so . . . how do I say? . . . so very obliging." And he winks knowingly.

Abe slumps back. He's a broken man. He fumbles restlessly in his pocket, draws out cigarette papers and a tobacco pouch. He rolls two joints, sullenly hands one to Mort. Bali's grade-A grass cures all sorrow. So the swingers light up and blow their desperate little minds all the way to Peliatan.

Our pink convoy draws up in a cloud of dust and disgorges. An unruly, foot-loose throng. Big-nosed, drip-dried, smelling of mutton. Intruders on alien soil, yet well chaperoned. We're met by a busy, black-tied manager from the hotel. Red tuxedo and all. He swaps our $1.50 stubs for Xerox copies of the program notes, then chivvies us to a three-deep crescent of canvas chairs. There's no stage, just a circle of beaten earth and a grassy slope. As a backdrop there's a graceful, ocher-swabbed temple, all snarling gods and curlicues. Behind us, discreetly kept back by ropes, the villagers have gathered, pointing, giggling, and gossiping.

"Oy, oy," shouts an Aussie. "We got the 'ole bloody mob tonight!"

His compatriots cheer. Impromptu.

"Good old 'Arry! Always got a friendly word for the peasants! The old bastard!"

The Aussies mill about like lost sheep. Mincing prettily, our Cockney fairy deftly intercepts Abe and Mort, nabs the Indian air hostesses. "Oh, you lovely things, you!" he gushes, and sits between them. The two swingers look downright wretched. I get 'Arry on my left, the widow from Pasadena on my right. 'Arry rolls up his nylon shirt sleeves, and the show begins.

Two young boys bring coconut shells filled with palm oil. They place them in a dead tree trunk, then light them. Across the moonlit meadow, a grave, silent assembly moves forward They are all men, and they are all naked. Except for a scarlet hibiscus behind the right ear and the briefest, indigo sarong. With quiet dignity, they settle around the dirt circle in five tightly packed, concentric rings. They sit cross-legged with their heads bowed. The oil lamps flicker, and their bodies glisten. Tight and lean.

"My gawd," sighs Mr. Kenneth. "Aren't they just too divine?"

For five long minutes, the men don't move. Not a muscle. Then abruptly, suddenly, to a split second, 150 voices bark in staccato chorus. It's electrifying. A wild sound, a jungle sound—

primitive, rough, untamed. *Chaka-chak-chaka-chak.* No gamelan gongs, not a single drum. Just 150 voices beating out a savage, contrapuntal tattoo.

Abe jerks up in his chair.

"Groovy!" he coos. And lights up two more joints of Bali's finest.

Chaka-chak-chaka-chak. Chak-chak-chak. Harsh, primeval. Fire-in-the-belly stuff. Then with a wrench, three hundred arms shoot upward, tossing in rhythm. *Chaka-chak-chak.* Bodies writhe, contorted. Rocking side to side. Fast, furious, unrelenting. *Chaka-chak-chak.* Between the mounting roar, a solo voice weaves a smoky, nasal plaint. And the chattering chorus responds, rapping up the beat. Driving, pounding, fiercely carnal.

The widow from Pasadena is chewing Spearmint, her mouth set in grimmest disapproval.

"Mercy! What on earth's going on?" she snorts.

I tell her it's a story from the *Ramayana.*

"Is that so? Well, they should know better, mister. Ain't never seen such a display in all my life!"

'Arry digs me in the ribs.

"Wot's the old cow bitchin' about now?" he growls. "'Ave a beer, mate!"

'Arry dips into his flight bag, opens six cans of Foster's Export.

Two girls flutter down the temple steps. Gliding, prancing, trailing veils of gauze, they slither between the sweating, panting chorus. *Chaka-chak-chaka-chak.* Fresh, innocent fawns trapped among half-crazed beasts. The men are meant to be monkeys, and they're doing fine. *Chaka-chak-chak.* They gibber and howl and grunt, bare their teeth, and gesture obscenely. Their claws strike out and paw the delicate girls, who twist and bob, then

Sumatra, the Golden Isle. Vast, empty, and extravagantly green. Deep in the highlands, the primal stillness is shattered by a silvery cascade tumbling cleanly down a sheer, mossy cliff into a limpid pool. A Batak traveler leads his yoked water buffalo. The big-wheeled oxcart, which can cross swollen rivers and pitted trails, serves as the voyager's bedroom, kitchen, and storehouse. Like Batak homes, the cart's roof slopes like the horns of a wild ox. This helps keep the demons at bay. ▶

sinuously escape. God only knows why. The program notes don't help. But it's stunningly, ferociously, hysterically exciting.

"Sock it to me, baby!" yells Abe, wreathed in smoke.

"I'm zonked, man!" hollers Mort. And he snaps his jellied fingers.

"Disgusting!" says the widow.

Chaka-chak-chak. Chaka-chak-chak. The noise is deafening, convulsive. My ears are throbbing. Bare backs trickle. Churning backward, forward, arms flailing, eyes flashing. Beneath scudding clouds, the palms bend and flutter in the wind. The oil lamps gutter. Three hundred arms rising and falling, tracing demonic spasms in the night. Thrusting, tugging. *Chaka-chak-chak.* Fabulous timing, phenomenally professional. Thrilling. Cruel. Raw. Hypnotic.

'Arry sinks his fifth beer. He's got bloodshot eyes, and they're drooping. Abe and Mort are bombed. Zap. Out of their minds. Mr. Yamamoto, three Nikons round his neck, pops up and down like a jack-in-the-box. The Indian girls smile politely, a stray pig nuzzles my feet, and Mr. Kenneth plainly forgets himself.

"Cripes! Twenty-fourth from the left! Fourth row! Isn't he smashing!"

Chaka-chak-chak. Chaka-chak-chak. The voices rage and roar, rise and fall. The girls twirl faster and faster. The monkeys scream. Fifteen hundred fingers flickering in the moonlight. *Chaka-chak-chak.* Backs arched, muscles twitching, shoulders swaying. Left, right, left. A flashing, stroboscopic frenzy of flesh and sound. A trip. A jungle jam session. *Walpurgisnacht.* God only knows. Then just as it started, it stops. Bang. Silence. A

◄ *Indonesia abhors banality, even in its fauna.* ABOVE: *A shaggy orangutan nibbles a scarlet hibiscus blossom with gourmet detachment. Actually he's cheating. He prefers salted cashew nuts. Trapped in Sumatra's rain forest, the orangutan viciously fought off his captors, yet he's grown tame and friendly as a puppy.* BELOW: *By contrast, the roosters are killers. At their roadside stall, a nonchalant couple sells fighting cocks. Once harmless enough, the roosters have been fed python blood, painstakingly massaged, and trained to kill. In Sumatra's many cockpits, they get fitted with razor-sharp steel spurs and fight to the death.*

hundred and fifty bodies lurch forward and collapse. Silence. Only the rustling of the palm fronds.

Most of us are too shaken to applaud. We just sit there, numb and exhausted.

"Man, I'm blowing my mind!" mumbles Abe and sinks limply into his chair. Up to the armpits.

'Arry is snoring. His tousled head has dropped on my shoulder.

"*Charmant, n'est-ce pas?*" says the retired French admiral.

"Yes. Very nice, wasn't it?" says the widow from Pasadena.

I decide it's high time to move on and out. Bali is a fine place to visit, but I wouldn't want to live here. As 'Arry would say, back to the bloody bush.

SUMATRA

■**1**■ It's one of Indonesia's minor paradoxes that the world's worst drivers should know how to fly planes at all. That they should do it well is little short of miraculous. Which is comforting, since our DC-3, a species I'd thought extinct, is on a twelve-hour milk run between meridians 117 and 98, where the seas are routinely described as "shark-infested." Still, I'm the only paleface on board, and I do wonder why.

Between Bali and Java, we'd had our outsiders. The schoolmarm from Chicago, catching a slow bus to Munich, via Delhi, Kabul, and places west. The ruffled Melbourne journalist who took six hours to fly into Timor and six weeks to get out. "We got stoned in Bali," said the hippie couple. "Yeah, they threw rocks at us." Yet even these adventurers abandoned the plane at Djakarta. With knowing smiles.

Now, hours later, we're dodging between boiling thunderclouds that flash mauve with soundless tropical lightning. Tail wiggling, clocking a jaunty 130 miles per hour, our jam-packed DC-3 scuds across the eerie emptiness of Sumatra. Not a road, not a village, not even a telltale curl of smoke. Just dark, mighty rivers winding like sluggish pythons over the horizon, and on every side, the rank, bottle-green jungle. As flat and unchanging as the Amazon basin.

Buffeted by the monsoon, we lurch and roll and shudder. Rain squalls crackle against the windows, and sometimes we drop sickeningly into oily space. We cross the equator, and my Chinese neighbor, who's chewing dried squid, says glumly: "Between Padang and Medan, no airfield. Only volcano and plenty bad people."

Sumatra is still one of the world's great virgin territories. After the crowding of Java and the harmony of Bali, it feels rough and wild, awesomely big, remote, and impenetrable. At the turn of the century, its Kubu tribes were still catching missionaries and broiling them for supper, and even today, a phone call from the capital can take two weeks or simply never happen. Between Banda Atjeh and Tandjung Karang, a cross-island jeep safari needs six weeks or more. The roads are appalling. The Dutch scratched the surface and little else. Sumatra, the Golden Isle, remains indescribably rich and unexploited. It is the Orient's Brazil.

And as we pitch and toss high above the black forests, time loses its purpose, my stomach turns inside out, and I wish I'd stayed home. But our pilot persists, and an infinity later, we dip suddenly, bounce viciously through swirling vapors, bank steeply, and touch solid concrete. My Chinese friend mops his brow, then bows with ceremony. "Buddha hear my speech," he says. "We lucky today." Maybe. But my knees feel like jelly, I've no hotel, no car, and I'm so shaken I can't remember why I came to Medan in the first place.

Anyway, Sumatra is open country. Wide open. If Java is Maugham, then Sumatra is Conrad. Boisterous, salty, untamed. And nowhere more so than Medan, just three degrees north of the equator, which retains all the raffish panache of a Conrad seaport. Like Malacca maybe, or Sarawak's Kuching. Even our limping DC-3 gets a welcome more fitting a China clipper.

In the warm, drizzling rain, there are flowered leis and tearful reunions, whole families hugging, paper streamers, and a brass band for the general. Trapped by the jostling mob, I feel groggy, depressed, and alone, when as happens in Indonesia, a swashbuckling trio elbows through the uproar, knocks over the barrier, asks my name, then hustles me through the prickly cordon of paratroopers and away. *"Selamat dalang!"* they chorus. "Welcome!" "We have car," says the first. "We have fun," says the second. "We have gun," says the third.

Who are they? God only knows. Seems the governor told them to meet me. Or was it a general? Or maybe they're meeting somebody else? But who cares? In Indonesia, it's wiser to keep quiet. Like the three monkeys.

Anyway, I've got a team once again, and thirty minutes later, we're settled at a grimy sidewalk table on Canton Road, drinking warm Bintang beer with ice cubes, dipping chopsticks into greasy bowls of noodles and salted pork. It's rowdy as hell. From a dozen porticoes, there's the gravelly shuffling of mahjongg blocks, while Chinese girls with bee-stung lips hustle in the back alleys, their *cheongsam* split to the thigh. Across the way, the street barber is pulling teeth with a pair of pliers, mongrel dogs roam like wolf packs, and a man tries to sell me an orangutan for seventy-five dollars. And scrambling between the tables, swarms of urchins hawking the newest shipment of smuggled goodies. American Winstons and Polish condoms, scent from Red China and aphrodisiacs from Japan.

Only one hour's flying time from Singapore, Medan flouts the law with frontier-town bravado and impunity. Its troops may be Indonesia's toughest, yet its customs officers are the most corruptly prosperous, its pimps the busiest, its gamblers the rowdiest, and its smugglers the most imaginative. Unlike Djakarta, Medan is raw, permissive, and cosmopolitan. It's also fun.

Medan has both a hulking mosque with sparrows in the rafters and a dainty, gilded Taoist temple, both gabled, eighteenth-century Flemish houses and a very British consulate. Royal crest and all. There are Chinese movies starring Ling Po and Chang Chung Wen as well as Hollywood's *Death Is a Woman*, billing Wayne Hickman, Zachary Hatcher, and other lost luminaries. Linking trim, grassy plazas, there are pockmarked avenues lined with eucalyptus and rows of cool, vaulted arcades painted ivory and built by the Dutch.

Skeletal Tamils with grave faces and bearded, pink-turbaned Sikhs; plump Indian ladies waddling in translucent saris; smiling Malays and crinkly-eyed traders from Foochow; dusty ragpickers and hollow-eyed waifs; farmers proudly wearing the black *kopiah* skullcap, Sukarno's trademark; Batak girls with waist-long plaits and spun-gold shawls; and swaggering

Lascar seamen who look like pirates and kick any Chinese rump in sight. And most places, an abundance of olive-green tanks, armored cars, and antiaircraft cannons that don't point at the sky. "Medan people sometime get too noisy," says Arifuddin, and picks his nose.

■ 2 ■

Our driver, Abdul, has a barrage of silver teeth and a brass knuckle-duster in his pocket. He blows his pay on bootleg liquor, gets drunk as a fiddler, and thinks our jeep is possessed by spirits. "Maybe good, maybe bad," he says. "I dunno." Abdul is Sancho Panza in Sumatra, but Arifuddin is a bore. He wears blue jeans, tooled Texas boots, and a bush ranger's hat. He's twenty-three, loud, obnoxious, and a student activist. A member of Suharto's New Forces, Ari never stops preaching nor asking questions. "Can I become a Black Muslim?" "Chinks are scum!" "Have you met Ava Gardner?" Ari is a bumptious twit, but you don't pick your companions in Indonesia. They simply materialize. Therefore I'm none too sure why we have a part-time gunslinger along, except that Ari keeps saying: "Batak people not so friendly," and that Arham, a morose beanpole who keeps his Colt in a canvas pouch, happens to be Ari's uncle.

In Djakarta, the townsfolk talk about Sumatra's Batak tribes in the same breath as the Dayak headhunters of Borneo, and Ari, who's been charged with my person, sounds chicken-hearted. "They eat dog and drink snake blood," he says. "They make plenty black magic." On which I tell him I haven't come to Sumatra to pick daisies, and we go.

Our jeep seems ready for the junk heap; yet as dawn breaks, we rattle with success through Medan's rush hour, past waking markets and drowsing paddies, then abruptly plunge into the primal rain forest. It's dark, dank, and smells of decay. Ari cockily swigs neat Cinzano from the bottle. Pea-green mists drift between monstrous ferns and clusters of sickly wild orchids, between rotting scrub and towering mahogany trunks that bleed crimson when scratched.

There's nothing nice about a jungle. Just pythons and leeches and clouds of mosquitoes, sweating boulders choked with moss and lichen, matted tangles of liana and thorny rattan untidily draped between sagging branches, scummy pools, and an oozing road speckled with mildew. We can't see the sky, and we haven't passed a car in three hours. In sharp, hairpin bends, we're climbing steeply. Our wheels slither, sometimes spinning helplessly. Our shirts are soaked. Yet mile by mile the jungle thins, dissolving into mountain firs and cedars, and finally we're clear. Abdul impetuously grabs the Cinzano and quaffs his share. "Spirito very kind today," he says.

Like India's Simla, Brastagi is a hill station built by colonials to escape the heat and flies. Fresh, breezy, and reasonably spruce, its pink and white bungalows have cozy names like Corner House and Bella Vista, recalling better days when pink-checked ladies played bezique and spaniels romped in the flower beds. Brastagi is a pleasant place—faded, genteel, and quite forgotten. On these verandas stolid burghers once sat tippling Bols, admiring the thrusting, volcanic heaps of Sibajak and Sinabung, which are both live, smoking, and uncomfortably close. But those were other times.

"We kick out Dutch," Ari says smugly. "Now *my* general makes party here." As do Japanese oil prospectors and other aliens, escaping the jungle for a morning's golf or a cool night's sleep. These days the deserted tennis courts are rank with weeds and the lawns need sprinkling; yet frisky ponies still canter down the twisting lanes, giant flame trees still shade the squares. And there's a friendly market where girls with flirty eyes perch behind neat pyramids of tangerines and pumpkin sized avocados, tending baskets piled with fruits whose shapes are as exotic as their taste. Sour *blimbing*, which look like starfish; sweet *durian*, plump and prickly as a porcupine; *apokat*, which taste like milk; *sawo*, which taste like bread; and juiciest of all, scaly *salak*, which seem wrapped in cobra skin but aren't.

Brastagi's market is humble in size, yet its prodigal diversity is astonishing—a token reminder that we've reached Sumatra's backbone, the golden highlands which are its wealth and fortune. And as we rough-ride across the rolling plateau, Suharto's "little back yard" explodes in all its grandiose affluence. From horizon to horizon, the vast forests and plantations multiply into infinity— a charmed landscape whose sheer enormity and richness are outrageous. But Ari couldn't care less. "Where do the Beatles live?" he asks.

Mile after mile, the tight ranks of oil, sugar, and sago palms, whole hillsides spread with pungent tea and coffee bushes, uncountable acres of cotton and tobacco leaf and razor-sharp pandanus. Hour after hour, thriving reserves of teak and 3,700 other timbers, unending rows of slender rubber trees bleeding into their tin cups. And in the distant ridges, lodes of silver and gold, untapped uranium, and gushing oil fields. The Golden Isle. A prodigious cornucopia of the world's riches. But Ari just picks his teeth. "How high is the Eiffel Tower?" he asks.

Unlike Bali, which is green and busy, the buff countryside is deserted. Maybe there are people, but they're neither working nor visible. Even the dust-caked villages seem abandoned. We haven't seen a face since Brastagi, when Arham wakes suddenly and begins oiling his Colt. "We coming Batak country," he says ominously. On which, like a stage cue, the sky darkens, lightning crackles, thunder claps, and the monsoon bursts. Our

Foolish fears and superstition. Framed by an intricately carved, coral-pink ▶
temple, three masked villagers pay cringing court to Ranga, queen of the
witches. Held up on towering stilts, the monstrous, yellow-maned demon,
played by another villager, screams, gibbers, and makes bloodcurdling in-
nuendoes. Although devoutly Hindu, most Balinese never overcome their
childish terror of ghosts, witches, and things that go bump in the night. As a
result, even adults prefer to sleep during daylight.

OVERLEAF: *The tranquillity of Bali. Under an enormous coolie hat, a young*
farmer gently chivvies his platoon of ducks past tidy tiers of ripening rice.
The sun pierces the clouds, and a refreshing drizzle spatters the road. Within
Bali there's a subtle, enchanting harmony between people and nature, as if
all conflicts had been settled centuries ago. The rice paddies, the temples, and
the people—they coexist peacefully. And this makes life both simple and
enjoyable. For their part, the ducks also comply. Once in their rice paddy,
they won't wander more than a few feet from their bamboo marker. In Bali,
"Order is Heaven's first law."

road, which had been better than some and worse than most, turns into slurping mud and a leaping army of frogs.

Abdul grinds into second, joyfully massacres the wildlife, and calls for Cinzano. In the sludgy, rain-swept half-light, we're apparently paddling upstream, but nobody's too sure. Abdul keeps missing corners, and the water's up to our hub caps. We're trapped in another maze of hairpin bends. Then Abdul brakes sharply. Very sharply. Our wheels are fortuitously poised on the edge of a cliff, and some 2,000 feet below, there's a lake. Squall-swept leagues of billowing water. And in the middle of the lake, there's an island, a formidable body of rock, a black and admittedly diabolical fortress. "Samosir!" cries Ari. "That's where they eat babies!"

3 Being a devout Muslim, Ari keeps a crumpled Koran in his hip pocket. He also eats pig, never fasts, and fairly swills back the hard stuff. "Times are changing," he assures me, and shamelessly bums another cigarette. Ari is the archetypal activist. He's insufferably opinionated and knows all the answers. Besides being a journalism student, he's also a mine of misinformation.

So despite his protests, I charter a boat next morning for "baby-eating" Samosir. Arham brings his gun and Ari a fresh bottle of Cinzano. With two glasses. The skipper, who's already gouged me for the ten-mile trip, charges an extra seventy-five cents a head for four inner tubes. Life belts, apparently, and he should know.

Our flaking hulk leaks atrociously, the engine splutters and chokes, and an early capsizal seems indicated. But I can swim

◀ *It's a festival day in Ubud, the painters' village, and a turbaned flower girl waits impassively for clients. Wrapped in her best sarong, she's selling bouquets fit for a god—orchids and hibiscus and heady frangipani, lovingly plaited with palm and pandanus leaves. "Won't you buy a flower off a poor girl, sir?" Not exactly. Unlike Eliza Doolittle, this flower girl has no hang-ups. She's in a thriving business. In Bali, religion is a peculiarly intimate affair, and the capricious gods must be placated daily. The demand for temple flowers is without end.*

and Ari can't, and anyway, Lake Toba is a wondrous discovery. Like Tahoe, Como, or Baikal, it's one of the world's great lakes. Almost 3,000 feet above the sea and sweeping fifty miles, its aquamarine waters, speckled with pirogues, fill an enormous volcanic crater. Circled by rakish cliffs and wooded bluffs, Toba has the texture of plate glass—a brittle mirror that reflects the clouds; and dead center there rises the proud table-mountain of Samosir, a somber, jungled heap laced with the silvery thread of tumbling cascades.

Samosir is the tribal home of the Batak people. From its shores, Si Raja Batak, the local Genghis Khan, swept across North Sumatra and established a ruthless, medieval dictatorship. His warriors butchered their prisoners and ate them, while captive chieftains were exquisitely tortured. Bamboo slivers were driven under their thumbnails; others were hung from meat hooks or simply fed cactus. At the turn of the century, the Batak still practiced devil worship, swallowed fire, and hunted missionaries for kicks. They were suspicious and remote, and a tribal taboo proscribed all outsiders from Samosir, the Sacred Island. Those who did come usually made a one-way trip, and the memory lingers on.

Yet as we wade barefoot to a pebbly beach, there is no volley of poisoned arrows, and Ari looks relieved. Just the buzzing of flies, sultry heat, and a few sullen glances. In Indian file, we trudge up a muddy trail past gaping, naked children; past a gloomy clutch of stone tombs and stark, graven images that recall Easter Island; past gaping, half-naked adults; and into the village of Ambarita, which seems barely to have stumbled out of the Stone Age. It's dirty, depressing, and slightly sinister. The moldy, wooden homes are built on stilts, the palm-thatched roofs are moss-grown, and the smell is terrible. Ari hits the Cinzano and asks me how to spell Marilyn Monroe. He's jumpy.

A bullock's skeleton bleaches in the hot sun, scrawny pigs snuffle between our feet, and a shrunken crone is gnawing a hunk of meat which looks suspiciously rare. The jungle crowds Ambarita on all sides, and I can feel we're being watched. The shadows track us silently, however, and Arham begins fingering his canvas pouch. Evidently the natives are not so friendly. Then between a cluster of plantains, I see a small, square clapboard shack with a cracked, stained-glass window. And jutting from the roof, a white cross.

I ask Ari. He looks confused, embarrassed. "Dunno," he mumbles. But Abdul, who has more sense, cups his hands and shouts out a dozen words. The jungle rustles and promptly parts on every side. The Batak villagers shuffle forward and encircle us. They examine me with awe, touch my clothes, and smile shyly. "*Horas! Horas!*" they keep saying. "You are welcome!" Against all odds, the shack is indeed a Christian chapel, and the quick-witted Abdul has told the restive villagers I'm a famed preacher from "distant lands."

Ari, the militant Muslim, reluctantly admits that the Batak *maybe* don't eat babies any more, but that much, much worse, they have become Christian. Since the thirteenth century, it seems, they had murderously resisted Islam, yet it took Pastor Nommensen, a stern Victorian missionary from Westphalia, only half a century to convert 900,000 fire-eating cannibals to his own obscure Lutheran sect. Possibly because Sumatra's version of Trust in God appears to tolerate the simultaneous worship of both the Holy Trinity, primeval mountain spirits, and one's ancestors' tombs.

Still, I'm uneasy in my new role as preacher-in-residence, but it's too late to retract. Flanked by a score of villagers, we're hustled to Ambarita's main square, an empty dirt space except for a monolithic, solid-rock table circled by seven equally monolithic, solid-rock thrones. In the misty past—there are neither dates nor calendars on Samosir— this was Si Raja Batak's council chamber, and rather apprehensively, I notice a familiarly shaped stone block. Oh, yes, says the village elder cheerfully, that's for executions. Since torture takes time, minor troublemakers had their heads chopped off promptly with a stone ax. And when did this custom lapse? Oh, maybe three generations ago. Hmm.

Seated in my stony armchair, I'm anxiously rehearsing an impromptu sermon, while Ari, the Muslim outsider, is ingratiating himself with the elders, rashly pouring whole tumblers of warm Cinzano. The patriarchs are getting merrily, if perilously, crocked when two wrinkled old ladies with betel-stained lips sidle close, bow devoutly, and hand me two dog-eared pocket books. The first is a hymnal printed in the Batak language and the second is a Bible, which amply quotes Raja David, Raja Solomon, and Protestant Kristus. The ladies invite me to sing a hymn. I decline politely. So they sing instead.

With reedy, croaking voices, they stand proudly erect, heads flung to the skies. I'll never know what they sang. Maybe "The Lord Is My Shepherd." But it doesn't matter. Their candor is infinitely touching. And when they finish, they smile nervously and kiss my hand. I thank them, yet intuitively sense they're expecting *something*. I don't know what to do. I feel deeply uncomfortable, as if I've somehow betrayed their innocent trust. So I fumble in my pockets, find two stray nickels, clumsily bless them, and place the coins in their hands. The old ladies beam happily, close their eyes, mumble a prayer, then walk the full three miles to our boat. As does the rest of the village.

And that evening, as we stroll by Toba's moonlit shore, Father Guido, a Franciscan missionary from Bombay, concedes that Samosir *is* a rather exotic outpost of Christianity. "We don't really know what goes on over there," he says. "But we're a bit suspicious." Besides hymn singing, he adds, the Batak flagrantly practice animism, worship rocks and trees, keep three wives or more. And when the moon changes, they hold wild, torchlight dances around their ancestors' tombs. For days on end. "How to keep them Christian at all?" Father Guido asks helplessly. "Samosir is strange enough. But if you strike south, things get curiouser and curiouser." So we do.

■4■ Down the lake, we're lodged in a verminous *losman*, a one-time Dutch inn. There are rats in the kitchen, the sheets smell moldy, and the toilets are horrendous. The place has evidently known better days, and an ancient ping-pong table stands forlornly in the patio. It's dank, drizzling, and damn depressing. I want bed.

But Ari lost a heap of face on Samosir, and he's still sulking. Brooding over his fifth beer, he knows he's somehow obligated. The infidel must be impressed. So Ari impetuously decides I must be shown the whorehouses of Parapat. It's Saturday night, after all.

"Parapat very famous for jigjig," Ari says airily, as our jeep splashes into this seedy, flaking township and draws up before a Chinese noodle shop. Ari drags me up creaking stairs into a musty, dimly lit chamber with three wooden partitions. Behind frayed curtains, there are wrestling shadows and a bit of grunting. The floors are unswept, a lantern blinks feebly, and a grubby white cat stalks between my legs. It has no tail.

Ari rubs his hands. "*Horas!*" he shouts. The sounds of creaking springs, and Ho Mei-ling, wrapped in a sateen kimono, trips out of the shadows. As her satisfied customer skulks through the doorway, Mei-ling bows politely—then smiles. She's got three front teeth missing, tired eyes, and she's picking nits out of her hair.

"You like?" Ari asks expectantly. But I don't. So we go to the Wismara instead.

This exotic knocking shop is carved out of a cliffside. It boasts a cobwebbed corridor, seven tacky rooms, and an outdoor privy. There are seven girls, seven boys; it's the Polly Adler's of Parapat.

Ari struts in like a pouter pigeon. "They know me," he says. "I come before. Only 250 *rupiah.* Short time." I assure Ari that sixty-five cents isn't exorbitant, and an unshaven, tubercular Batak chivvies us past two gents chatting in their underpants and into a cubicle. There's a striped mattress on the floor, a dented spittoon, and a single, naked light bulb. Once again, no door. Just a stained cotton curtain. Very cozy.

Ari stretches out on the mattress. With his boots on, he reclines extravagantly, every inch the tin-pot pasha. Ari claps his hands. We sip our cold tea; then the curtain divides, and Hartika, the house favorite, waddles in. She's pimply, blacker than molasses, and her jellied bounties are only loosely contained by a turquoise, crepe de chine negligee. Hartika settles around Ari like kneaded dough, nuzzles his ear, and betel juice dribbles down her chins. She's so ugly I could scream.

"Nice girl, don't you think?" Ari says unctuously.

I try to look cheerful, but I'm clearly not convincing. Blubber isn't my kind of meat. So Ari claps again. The tubercular Batak reappears, there's a mumbled exchange, and a few minutes later, two scrawny, barefoot young girls shuffle hesitantly through the curtain. They blink their eyes, bewildered by the harsh light.

Their bony bodies protrude through cheap batik shifts. Their drawn cheeks are rouged, their lips painted, and brass bangles tinkle sadly from their wrists. They can't be over twelve. Ari talks with them harshly, then snorts.

"It's no good, *tuan*. One is pregnant. The other has the disease."

Ari stubs his cigarette on the floor. He suddenly looks angry.

"Take Hartika," he says impatiently, and pushes her towards me. The girl flops a suety hand on my knee, then grins vacuously. Her fingernails are filthy, she smells rancid, and her breath would stun a polecat.

Sorry, says the infidel.

I want to throw up.

Ari's brows arch in astonishment. He's mortified, I do believe.

5 At breakfast Ari asks me who was Jesus Christ's grandmother, and this time he's gone too far. If he asks one more question, I'll brain him. So since it's Advent Sunday, I decide to subvert my Muslim trio and take them to church. Which in Sumatra is sooner said than done.

The shores of Toba are glutted with hundreds of tiny, steepled boxes, but their timetables are as haphazard as the doings inside. Many chapels haven't opened their doors in a decade, others open only for Easter, and in most cases, services just happen—usually when villagers and preacher are ready for a convivial singsong. "It's not quite like elsewhere," says our Batak guide, Djamal, who's both Christian and a college graduate.

We clamber up hillsides, and the chapels are firmly padlocked; we edge down cliffside paths, and the rough-cut pews are crawling with wild cats. We find one chapel crammed with nit-picking Batak women. They squat in the aisles suckling babies, smoking cigarettes, and scratching their dogs. We're driving south from

Toba across sere, empty scrub, and Ari looks smug. Forty, sixty, eighty miles. Catholic, Lutheran, Adventist—they're all closed. I'm getting to feel foolish; then we hit Balige, a scruffy, one-story market town, and it might as well be Mardi Gras. "Time for church," says Djamal.

Oxcarts strewn with flowers and gaudy pony traps, ramshackle buses with feather pennants and swarms of tinkling cycles, boys riding buffaloes and hobbling old men. Young girls with brocaded sarongs and frangipani in their hair, old men in sober indigo batik, mothers balancing Bibles on their heads and babies on their backs, dogs, pigs, goats, and scampering roosters. An eddying procession which drifts leisurely and cheerfully, as if going to a revel rather than holy worship.

We're soon swept up by the barefoot, jostling parade and ten minutes later get squeezed into the organ loft. Djamal tactfully removes Arham's gun from the pew and asks Ari to take off his slouch hat. The whole church is built of costly teak, immaculately polished. Women sit on the right, men on the left. Behind the altar, the vault shimmers with an enormous Byzantine mural of Jesus with the Batak legend "Kristus Is Ready; He Welcomes All." In black, pinched shoes and a shiny suit, the Batak preacher faces his flock, then raises his arms like a maestro; everybody stands, and suddenly one thousand voices ring out in unison. It's deafening, thrilling, and utterly extraordinary.

There's nothing tame about Batak devotions. Six trumpets, three drummers, two organs which risk bursting their pipes, and the music can be heard three miles away. Inside the church, the pews vibrate and the windows rattle. The cataracts of sound are almost intolerable. Pounding, barbaric hallelujahs which numb the senses, and every head raised high, as if they're singing their souls straight to Heaven. Between the hymns, the husky preacher rips off his coat and attacks his brethren with apocalyptic, Bible-pounding fury. "Do you believe?" he roars. "Yes, yes, yes!" they roar back. "Who do you believe?" "Kristus, Kristus, Kristus!" The most rip-roaring kind of evangelism, as jubilant as a hot gospel chorus, and Ari is flabbergasted. "How much does it cost to become Christian?" he asks.

For my part, I'm also overwhelmed. This may not be religion, but the massed choir's vibrancy and fervor is a knockout. It's better than Verdi's *Requiem*. That these simple Batak should show such blind, undemanding faith in an alien religion imported from halfway around the world is something else. "You've just seen one side of the coin," says Djamal. "They may be Christians now, but they'll be demon-haunted pagans by nightfall." So our guide, who hasn't been home for ten years, impulsively suggests a trip to his own remote Batak village. "Don't worry," he adds. "They live in the Stone Age. But they're *also* Christians!"

■6■ After three bone-crunching hours driving between empty, ragged hillsides, we dip into a valley and the track simply stops. There's no road to Lumban Lubu, not even a path. So we walk, sloshing and squelching across the flooded rice fields, stumbling dejectedly through the loamy, oozing mud. There's nothing melodramatic about walking into the Stone Age. The muck is up to our knees, Ari wants to go home, and we're all drenched in sweat. Then Djamal finds a narrow dike and points into the hazy distance. Isolated in time and space, Lumban Lubu perches on a palm-tufted knoll, a lost island floating between water-logged paddies.

Like tightrope walkers, we sidle across four bamboo poles that bridge the village stream, and since I'm the first paleface ever to call, Arham glumly drops six slugs into his Colt. But it's a sham, I know. In Indonesia, guns aren't weapons that kill; they're just amulets which scare off devils. They might as well be plastic.

"Come quietly," says Djamal and escorts us down a sludgy, overgrown track, through thorny tangles of brushwood, and into a clearing. Behind low, stone walls, a dirt quadrangle, and a dozen Batak homes. The houses are dark, primitive, and

The aplomb of centuries. Under a waxed parasol, a slim, dusky beauty and her daughter wait for time to pass. Is the bus five hours overdue? Has daddy run off again? Has uncle been busted as a Communist? No matter. Mother's stoicism will carry the day. After all, she's been married since she was thirteen.

wooden; they're built on thick stilts, hooded with mildewed thatch that curves like the horns of the *banteng* wild ox. The village is deserted.

Djamal calls out. Clouds of insects buzz the fetid puddles, but there's no welcoming reply. Buffalo skulls and grisly clusters of dried snakes hang in the porches; the walls are carved with macabre ghouls and demons, snarling tigers, and rampaging panthers. The spirits are evidently kept at bay, but the silence is unnerving. Lumban Lubu is musty, secretive, and smells of death.

"Horas!" calls Djamal, and his voice echoes emptily between the somber, spectral homes. In the dank heat, the stillness is oppressive, almost hostile. Djamal seems apprehensive. Then, from the shadows, a stooping, withered creature appears. He wears a grimy sarong and a turban and a necklace of leopard teeth, limps painfully on a stick. Actually he's thirty-seven, Djamal's elder brother, and the village chief.

His jaundiced eyes examine Djamal gravely; then he speaks: "Many years ago you went away. Now you must leave again. Instantly." The prodigal son looks abashed, shuffles uneasily. He knows he's broken the tribal law—"There is no return to the village"—but Djamal isn't intimidated. He replies firmly, sharply, and his brother's eyes slowly switch to me, flicker uncertainly, then fill with wonder. Without thinking, I quickly hand him the two handkerchiefs I'd bought as gifts in Balige, and the chief drops to his knees. It seems hardly credible, but Djamal has glibly told his brother that I am the reincarnation of Paster Nommensen. "I have nothing to give you, *tuan*," says the awe-struck chief, "but may God send you blessings forever." And he touches my hand. In Indonesia, the visitor plays many parts.

From all sides, the hiding villagers shuffle into the hot, daz-

◀ *Quo vadis? Now there's a question. In Indonesia, people don't travel. They improvise movements. On this occasion, they're going nowhere, just pottering. It's the hour before dusk. Squatting in rough, dugout canoes, these Batak villagers cool off on the glittering waters of Lake Toba. The boy with the bicycle gazes smugly at the shore. The rusting cycle belongs to his elder brother, who is not amused.*

zling sunlight. They're emaciated, half-naked, and clearly bemused. Three women bring me babies to baptize; another fumbles spellbound with my ballpoint pen, as if it were a sacred relic. The chief says that the buffalo skulls help keep the devils away but that Kristus is a far more powerful deity, then invites me up the ladder into his home.

Just a single room with smoke-blackened walls. Hand-made raffia mats for sleeping and hand-made wooden hoes for the fields. A crude hand loom for weaving and a hand-carved flute for music, palm-fiber baskets, and sewing needles made from bone. For light, a coconut husk filled with palm oil and for cooking, a block of stone and a charcoal fire. Stone pots brimming with flyblown lard and stone dishes stacked with yams. No axes, no hooks, not even a metal knife. Just the crudest implements of a neolithic society that can neither read nor write. Here time has stopped. On this island refuge, the people have never seen a newspaper nor heard a radio. They speak their own archaic dialect and don't use money; and the women do the work. All of it.

"We are all fine Christians," the chief says proudly and hands me Lumban Lubu's most treasured artifact, a bookworm-riddled Bible printed in Hamburg, 1903. And maybe to confirm his piety, he takes me to the edge of the village and shows me the tribal mausoleum, a solid, mud-brick pile topped with a rough-cut wooden cross. "If there's sickness or the harvest fails," says Djamal, "they remove the bones, carry them into the village, and polish them. At nightfall they light bonfires, then dance around the heaped bones. They pray to our ancestors, placate the demons with gifts, sacrifice a live pig or two."

Back in the village square, Djamal's brother, who doubles as preacher and witch doctor, solemnly invites us to a timeworn rock table with matching rock seats. The women serve banana leaves heaped with cold, boiled rice, which we eat with our fingers, and split coconut shells of home-brewed *tuak*, a palm wine which makes tequila taste like a milk shake. Still it's a relaxed party, and even Djamal seems forgiven, when all at once, there's a spine-chilling shriek, and across the way, a woman tumbles out of a Batak house, pitches down the ladder, and collapses in twitching convulsions. Ari gapes open-mouthed and drops his coconut.

Djamal questions his brother urgently, then pulls my sleeve. We climb the front steps, duck through the waist-high doorway, and enter a darkened room. Blood-red devil masks hang from the walls, and a dozen villagers crouch around an inert and naked body stretched out on a palm-weave mat. They moan and weep, tears flooding their cheeks, then abruptly burst into delirious, hysterical laughter. "It's the custom," says Djamal. "A death watch." At times the sobbing mourners rise unsteadily, circle the body with slow, ritual steps, then groggily hit the floor. The room reeks of *tuak*, and everybody is intoxicated, probably doped. The heat is stifling and the stench indescribable.

The corpse has been here forty-three days.

7 "How did you like my family?" Djamal asks dryly, but I'm too shaken to reply. I want to get out of the Stone Age now and forever. I need fresh air. So I throw the jeep into gear, and as the afternoon shadows deepen, we blast through Balige, where the choirs are still rejoicing, and strike randomly into the mountains. On every side, the dun, leathery foothills are speckled with white—the squat, chalky outlines of Batak mausoleums with their tidy Christian crosses and the polished bones within. Tombs inspired by the alien Kristus, tombs that open and shut with demoniac informality. "And where are *your* ancestors' bones, Mr. Lucas?" asks Ari.

Djamal tells him to shut up, then directs me down a rutted, dusty track, across a wide plateau scorched by brushfires, past mud holes where buffaloes wallow, past bleak villages with corrugated roofs, past galloping herds of hungry wild ponies. "Huta Gindjang," says Djamal without comment. The track corkscrews steeply between volcanic boulders and forests of ferns, climbs above the tree line into a wasteland of cinnamon crags, cuts through precipitous bluffs and soaring buttresses. Wedged between walls of rock, the track turns into crumbling slabs of lava. Our wheels spin, churning and splintering the brittle texture. Higher, higher, higher. The air grows chilly,

In Indonesia, there is no neutral gray. Only white and black. It's a country where adventure still lives, where the most lunatic improbability becomes fact, where there's only a razor's edge between comedy and disaster. It's a territory where life, like art, is still raw and real. It violates the senses. Indonesia is funny, spontaneous, bizarre, charming, exotic, improvised, and utterly exhausting. It's a land where indifference is impossible. You get involved. Inescapably so.

Indonesia is a happening.

■9■ Huta Gindjang. Misty, ethereal, remote. It's a pity my trip won't end here. It's both a sane and a beautiful place. But perverse Indonesia abhors such balance. My trip won't end this day, or the next, or the next. Instead, we'll clatter back to Parapat, where the whores are still lousy with lice; we'll drive wearily back to Medan, where the orangutan now costs only twenty-five dollars, and where Ari asks me, please, to write. And one steamy morning, I clamber into the DC-3, strike southeast across the equator, and return to musty, miserable Djakarta.

Nothing has changed. The streets still swirl with dust; the palms look wretched; and the troops are back in the hotel kitchen. Six weeks ago, they came for sandwiches and a pint of tea. Tonight, a whole paratroop platoon breaks in, machine guns dangling. This time, they want turkeys, lobsters, and roasts of beef.

With nonchalant aplomb, the paratroopers spray a few casual bursts into the kitchen ceiling, drive the cook-boys into a corner, shoot off the Swiss chef's hat, fill up their canvas sacks, then walk away. Outside the dining room, the chef slumps into a red velvet armchair. His face is ashen, and his eyelids twitch. "The Gstaad Palace," he says weakly, "was never like this."

Maybe. But who gives a damn? I'm getting out tomorrow. 0745 hours. Garuda flight 872. If nothing else, I've come to terms with kismet. Check. Double check.

Indonesia is a happening.

FOR THE RECORD

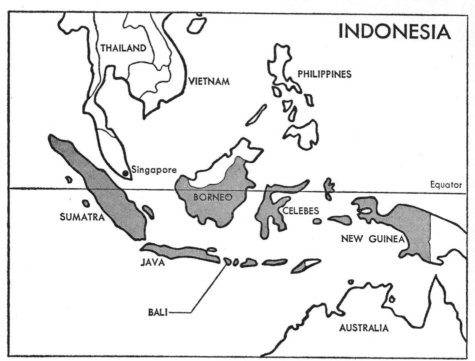

INDONESIA

THAILAND

VIETNAM

PHILIPPINES

Singapore

BORNEO

CELEBES

SUMATRA

NEW GUINEA

JAVA

Equator

BALI

AUSTRALIA

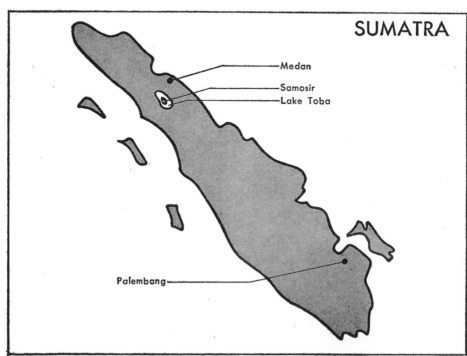

SUMATRA

Medan

Samosir

Lake Toba

Palembang

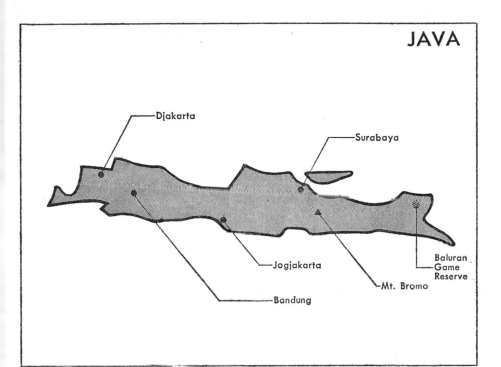

JAVA

Djakarta

Surabaya

Jogjakarta

Bandung

Mt. Bromo

Baluran
Game
Reserve

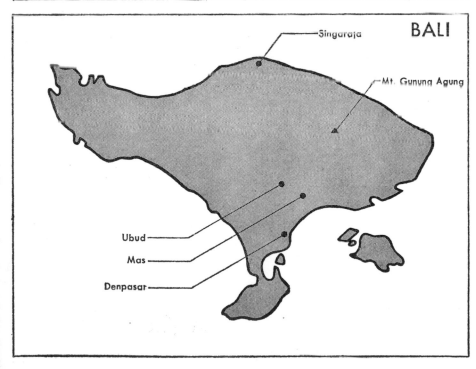

BALI

Singaraja

Mt. Gunung Agung

Ubud

Mas

Denpasar

GLOSSARY OF TERMS

Batik: Dyed cloth produced in Java. A funnel-like device (or, more recently, a stamp) is used to coat cotton cambric with molten wax except for the places to be dyed. The process of coating and dyeing is repeated many times to create a multicolored design. High-quality batik can take up to six months to prepare.

Gamelan: Orchestra of Bali and Java, usually composed of about twenty-five players. Instruments include gongs, metallophones, xylophones, and the violinlike *rabab*. Compositions last about fifteen to thirty minutes. There are some fifteen kinds of gamelans for dramas, concerts, funerals, dances, and other events. Playing technique is handed down through successive generations; there is no written score.

Garuda: Mythological golden eagle, a common motif in Indonesian art. Also used in the nation's state seal. A manifestation of the Hindu god Vishnu the Preserver.

Kain: Finished length of material nine feet long and four feet wide. Worn by both men and women, it is fastened at the waist by a sash. A *kain* with *kebaya* is the native costume of Indonesian women.

Kebaya: Jacket with long, close-fitting sleeves made of cotton (the wealthy use silk or velvet). Worn with a sarong or *kain* and topped by a *slendang* (shawl).

Ketjak: the so-called Monkey Dance. Some 150 men wearing loincloths crouch in concentric circles around an oil lamp, swaying and chanting. The story concerns the monkey armies of Hanuman and Sugriwa, figures from the *Ramayana* who help rescue King Rama's wife.

Kuda kepang: Trance dance of East Java using cutout, bamboo-weave hobbyhorses. The musical group usually consists of gongs, a drum, and a flute. After the music begins, the dancers go into a trance convinced they are horses. In many

15th century: Islamic kingdoms grow up around Majapahit, initially recognizing its suzerainty. Later Majapahit declines, its Muslim vassal princes revolt, and the Majapahit court flees to Bali (1478).

16th century: Portuguese arrive in Indonesia (1509) and seize Muslim state of Malacca (1511). First Dutch ships arrive in Java (1596).

17th century: Dutch East India Company, created in 1602, founds Batavia as a trading base (1619) and takes over control of Malacca (1641). Fighting occurs between Dutch and local sultans.

18th century: Dutch East India Company gains political power through agreements with local rulers. Later the company collapses and transfers its territories to the Dutch government (1799).

19th century: British briefly hold Indonesia (1811–16). Dutch enforce system of compulsory cultivation (1831–77). Native revolts erupt but are suppressed.

20th century: Paternalistic "ethical policy" instituted (1901). Various nationalist groups arise and protest Dutch rule. Following Japanese occupation (1942–45), Sukarno proclaims Indonesia's independence, but Dutch grant sovereignty only after U.N. intervention (1949). In 1965, the increasingly Peking-oriented rule of Sukarno toppled by General Suharto. The current doctrine is called *Pantja Sila*, or the Five State Principles: Belief in One Supreme God, Civilized Humanity, Nationalism, Democracy, and Social Justice.

The "weathermark" identifies this book as having been planned, designed, and produced at the Tokyo offices of John Weatherhill, Inc. Book design and typography by Meredith Weatherby. Text composed and printed by General Printing Company, Yokohama. Plates engraved in five-color offset and printed by Nissha Printing Company, Kyoto. Bound at the Makoto Binderies, Tokyo. The text is set in Monotype Bell eleven point, with hand-set Nile for display.